Advance praise for
A Republic of Trees

"We are in need of new technologies, yes, but even more in need of new  ng the very smartest p of social and environr e we'll be relying on i

— Bill McKibben
author of *The End of Nature*
and *Deep Economy: The Wealth of Communities
and the Durable Future*

"There is more insight and vision packed into this little volume than in the last five books I've read."
— Mark Dowie
author of *Losing Ground: American
Environmentalism at the Close of the Twentieth
Century* and *American Foundations: An
Investigative History*

"A Republic of Trees is a bold, timely collection that makes accessible Shutkin's unique insights as a leading environmental social entrepreneur, lawyer, and educator. A Republic of Trees is a must-read for all those who believe or wish to believe that a green and just world is possible and a primer on how to get there."
— Cheryl L. Dorsey, President, Echoing Green

...more advanced praise

"*A Republic of Trees* is a powerful work that's striking for its grace, humility, and gentle persuasion. In challenging us to create a more sustainable future, Bill Shutkin doesn't scold but appeals to our better nature. His book is a worthy successor to Aldo Leopold's classic *A Sand County Almanac.* Shutkin argues that it's no longer enough to think like a mountain; we must think like a city, a nation, a planet."

— David Baron
NPR Science Reporter
and author of *Beast in the Garden:
A Modern Parable of Man and Nature*

"As with the writings of John Berger, Bill Shutkin's words harmoniously resonate with, and reconcile, a hard-worked land; a land encumbered by fragile communities, bestowed with a sacredness by many, divided by geology and rivers, saturated with the sweat of field labor, and shaped by hard weather or polluted soils and the corrosive power of real estate. Shutkin's 'Field Notes' mend scars in this landscape, weaving paths, and carefully uniting human detail and vegetation with contour lines, agricultural patterns, rock and human formations and always searching for a sense of the sense of the enduring continuity of people and place."

— Niall Kirkwood
Professor and Chair
Department of Landscape Architecture
Harvard University

A Republic of Trees

Field Notes on People, Place, and the Planet

William Shutkin

The Public Press

Randolph Caspar

Library of Congress Cataloging-in-Publication Data
Shutkin, William.
A REPUBLIC OF TREES.
I. Title.
ISBN 978-0-9764520-8-9

Cover image: "Winter Woods" by Sabra Field

Acknowledgments

You could say this book itself is an acknowledgment. I was motivated to undertake it by a desire to see these writings, most of which will have been seen or heard by a relatively small audience over roughly the last decade, brought together under a single cover. My aim in doing this is not only to preserve them in a single place, giving them a second life in the process, but to acknowledge a particular period of my life—both professional and, ineluctably, personal--captured in them.

These are not all of my published writings from the period, but they more or less cover the bases. I've omitted some that were either too long, such as law review articles or book chapters, or were duplicative of the pieces I've included. I've also chosen to include three keynote addresses, two of which were published by the sponsoring organizations in their newsletters or magazines. Over the past decade, I've delivered over 50 keynotes and public lectures; the pieces in this volume are loosely representative of many of these.

As I sit here in a writing cabin at the Mesa Refuge in Point Reyes, California, watching a hummingbird sip at the stout Foxglove arrayed before my window, I realize I've reached a stage of my life and career one might call a milestone. For the past 15 years, beginning in my late 20s, I've tried to use my skills as a lawyer, educator and social entrepreneur to promote environmental protection and sustainable communities. To date, I've led three organizations engaged in the effort to put the environment foremost in the minds and actions of people and institutions, alongside other priorities such as social equity and economic opportunity. Meanwhile, I spent a good deal of this period teaching at the graduate level, in both a law school and an urban planning program, to train and mentor the next generation of environmental professionals equipped with the sensibility, skills and energy to take on the new kinds of challenges twenty-first century environmentalism presents them.

I believe we are witnessing wholesale changes in not only the way we approach environmental problems but, more interestingly, the way we think about them, less as a specialized area of inquiry and policy led by experts trained in law, the sciences and engineering and more as an interdependent field embedded in, if not underlying, all other knowledge and policy areas (which explains the play on the word "Field" in the book's subtitle). In turn, I believe these changes require a new cadre of environmental professionals— from the grassroots to the highest echelons of government and industry—armed not only with new tools but a new understanding about the very nature of the work they're doing.

Over the past decade and a half, I've been fortunate to actually see environmental concerns take center stage. As never before, issues such as climate change, sustainable agriculture, sprawl, green building and renewable energy have begun to stir, if not plain rattle, the hearts and minds of the American public. Environmental quality is now invoked as a companion, and not a competitor, to social policy goals such as job creation and affordable housing. That the word "green" has become a commonly used verb is no small sign of the environment's ascendance as a seminal social issue. While by no means tackled, environmental challenges enjoy a currency and visibility unlike at any other time in U.S. or, for that matter, human history. In parallel with my career, environmental policy and politics have arrived at a discrete moment in time, a tipping point, at which we've come to approach them with a heightened level of consciousness, gravity and, most importantly, possibility.

A Republic of Trees is a record of a distinct period of

thought and action in my life, a particular body of work recognizable by a shared set of themes, ideas and sentiments that might well, over time, evolve or shift, or perhaps, in hindsight, even prove misguided, but that, nevertheless, reflect not only my own outlooks and insights at the time but the historical context with which they are bound up.

Speaking of bonds, the writings in this collection and the book itself are a product of a raft of relationships with people, organizations and places I have known. Some are mentioned explicitly, many others are found between the lines or are part of the backstory. I want to acknowledge their contribution. These include the dozens of friends and colleagues who have generously reviewed and shared their thoughts on my work over the years. A special thanks are owed to two of these, John Fox and Karen Yacos. We are all, to some extent, nothing more than the sum of other peoples' attitudes, beliefs and insights or, as Wallace Stegner put it, "every idea rests upon other ideas that have preceded it in time." All intellectual work is a cumulative, collective effort. This one is no different.

I also want to thank Peter Barnes, Mark Dowie, Harriet Barlow, Chris Desser, Pam Carr and the Mesa Refuge for allowing me the time and space to pull this collection together, and to my retreat mates, Michael Pollan and Andi McDaniel, for their friendship and solidarity. No doubt they are each contributors well beyond providing an extraordinary work space, but having the ability to step back, see one's work and life anew and produce, which the Mesa Refuge uniquely affords, is a singular gift, akin to the gift of time itself.

Thanks are owed as well to Stephen Morris and The Public Press. Stephen and I first met in San Francisco many years ago when we were both attending separate conferences on social enterprise literally around the corner from each other. Stephen was still in the process of pitching the Press as a business concept and I was intrigued. A talented and creative entrepreneur, Stephen has provided a unique service for writers whose work might otherwise slip through the cracks of more conventional publishing houses. In my case, a collection of writings from an author without a large readership is almost a non-starter from a commercial publishing perspective. The Public Press is an open source, on-line infrastructure for such authors, enabling the production and distribution of all sorts of fiction and non-fiction works that would otherwise wither away in the abject obscurity of a dusty file cabinet or bottomless hard drive.

A special thanks to Sabra Field, with whom I collaborated on a unique project in 2007 called "Reimagining Vermont: A Conversation with Sabra Field and William Shutkin about the Future of Vermont's Landscapes and Livelihoods." The spirit and content of that project were informed by and, in turn, informed several pieces in *A Republic of Trees*, excerpts from which were part of our "conversation." As someone who believes that art, and artists, are powerful prophesiers, designers more like it, of an otherwise unknowable future, I have looked to Sabra's insights and imaginings, expressed in her colorful images, as a source of inspiration. Her prints inhabit that risky but exciting space between the world as it is and as it might be.

I'm grateful, too, to the many editors who have supported the work found in this collection, among them Heather Boyer and Chuck Savitt, Steve Curwood, Stephen Long, David Moats, Jonathan Moyers, Marjorie Pritchard, William Saunders, Betty Smith and Aki Soga. Thanks, too, to the editors of Grist, Urban Ecology and Mute Magazines.

Finally my deepest thanks go to Sally Handy and our children, Olivia and Shepard, for their love, support and flexibility in allowing me the time and privilege of putting this book together. I wrote and compiled *A Republic of Trees* in large part to be able to give to my children a volume they could hold in their hands, a disembodied, discrete product they could refer to as they grow older, begin to interrogate the world and establish their own careers, causes and beliefs. Unmediated by the inflections or emotions of an actual conversation, I hope this book will serve as a source of information and insight about their father's ideas and opinions and the times in which he, and they, lived. Should they choose, I want them to learn from what I have tried to do in my career, take the game to the next level and become part of that elusive intergenerational feedback loop, the fragile and all-too-rare transmission of knowledge from one generation to the next, not just for their benefit, but of those to follow.

Point Reyes Station, California
June 2007

To Sally, Olivia and Shepard,
a big part of my small world

And to Vermont and California, states of mind
(to borrow a line from the late historian Robin Winks)
and the two cherished places where much of this volume
was written and assembled

Introduction

A Republic of Trees is both a precursor and sequel to my
first book, *The Land That Could Be: Environmentalism and
Democracy in the Twenty-First Century*. Several pieces in *A
Republic of Trees* were written before *The Land That Could Be*
was published in 2000, most came after, but all engage or
build on the key themes and concepts discussed in that book
in some meaningful way, starting with the title.

As with *The Land That Could Be*, the title for this volume,
taken from one of the pieces in the collection, reflects my on-
going intellectual and professional quest to align natural and
human-made systems into one unified, bold and sustainable
model for social and economic development. Just as the *Land*
in the title of my earlier book was meant to suggest as yet
unrealized ecological and social possibilities – Land as Nature
and Nation – this volume's title is equal parts environmental
metaphor and social change proposal. As metaphor, trees
are a powerful proxy for people, at once individuals and
community members, complex and straightforward,
producers and consumers, natives and migrants, of all shapes,
sizes and colors. Trees as people. Now imagine a political
order, a republic – of, for and by the people (from the Latin,
res (thing) and *publica* (people)) – concerned equally with its
people and its trees, in which society and nature are seen as
interdependent, as nourishing and sustaining eachother in a
perpetual process of social and ecological development. A new
republic, a Republic of Trees.

At its core, my career, like that of any social change agent,
has been about creative destruction, about the process of

establishing a new order by dissolving an old one. In this case, the old order is the binary framework through which we've come to view the relationship between nature (trees, wetlands, wilderness and the like) and society (the cultural, political and economic practices and institutions that give order and meaning to our lives) and the host of other relationships associated with it – industry/ecology, urban/ rural, black/white, local/global, private/public, I/we. I believe such a framework has long outlived its useful life in helping us understand and organize reality in a way that optimizes the health and well-being of not only people, but their places and the planet as a whole. As an alternative, I've chosen to imagine the world in ecological terms, as one continuous, interconnected system comprised of countless intricately designed parts, each in some way constituting or giving shape to the other and, in the process, forming one, universal commons of mind and matter.

From the natural and social sciences to the humanities, from government to business, from the industrialized world to the industrializing, this view is starting to take root, starting to undermine the old structures and ways of understanding the world that have for centuries, at least in the West, pitted economies against ecology, culture against nature, us against them. Unlike just a generation ago, today with a straight face we can talk about green buildings from Boston to Beijing, about African immigrants across rural America, about green roof tops and farmers markets in our mega-cities, about wind farms in the Texas oil patch and China's coal country and about struggling Rust Belt businesses starting to compete again, on-line, in the new global marketplace.

We have entered a new era, defined not by rigid hierarchies and categories, not by clear lines of difference, but by collapsing ones, progressively pervious borders between what was and what will be, between ecology and culture, between us and them. Though the destination remains uncertain, and the route decidedly non-linear, today we are all migrants entering once forbidden cultures, markets and disciplines, and at speeds as fast as our imagination and a broadband connection will carry us. In turn, we are all collaborators, however unwilling, in building a new kind of transcendent, some might say cosmopolitan, experience and sensibility, a new kind of connected, global commons arising out of the heap of toppled borders.

A Republic of Trees is a field guide to this emergent new commons, a personal chronicle, in fits and starts, of our evolving understanding regarding the relationship between nature and society and its companion "either/or" constructions. Written largely though not exclusively from a New England perch, with its own particular people and places, the book presents perspectives and themes unbounded by context or jurisdiction. This is in keeping with the book's central premise that we inhabit a planet increasingly defined by our shared destiny, not our differences, where the distance between continents has been reduced to a keystroke and the gap between disparate sets of data, once rendering a fragmented picture of reality, has been closed by technologies that allow us to analyze and visualize the world in its many dimensions – social, economic, ecological – all on a single computer screen. The globe, in other words, has never been smaller or more tightly connected than it is today, an unfolding continuum of interlocking experience and consciousness, much of it brought to us, perhaps paradoxically, by a machine.

The book is designed as an interlocking set of parts. Comprised of over 60 essays, op-eds, commentaries, blogs and speeches published between 1998-2007, it is divided up into three nested meta-themes – People, Place and the Planet – constituting discrete, though overlapping, sections that, together, create a coherent whole.

Part I, People, is the inner-most circle in the nest. It addresses issues of governance, civic engagement, cultural diversity and demographics. It explores questions such as, How in a pluralistic society do we reconcile our different opinions and points of view so as to govern ourselves and our environment effectively? And, How do individuals transform the I into We, arguably humanity's most formidable barrier, to realize a shared vision of the possible?

Place, Part II, examines the idea, experience and practice of place and place-making, one step removed from the People circle. It responds to questions such as, How do we give meaning to places? And, What's the nature of place in a globalizing, increasingly borderless age?

Part III, the Planet, is the outermost ring, exploring the ways in which people and place combine to shape or change the natural environment. It takes on the matter of climate change, capitalism and the environmental movement. It examines the bigger picture, where the small meets the large, attempts to redescribe global challenges as tractable, personal issues and speaks to the seminal, age-old problem of collective action.

In organizing the book this way, my aim is to bring some imperfect, though artful, order to the chaos of dozens of writings produced over a ten-year span, knowing that, in one way or another, they are all of piece, all stem from the same source, all point in a similar direction.

And direction is what I'm after. While I espouse the idea that much of human evolution is incremental, non-linear and, as the Harvard paleontologist Stephen J. Gould reminded us, punctuated, I also have a sense that, owing to the very forces – technological, economic, social and environmental – responsible for breaking down barriers of knowledge, culture and geography, we are poised to accelerate the pace of human evolution to a point where the ideal of a truly just, unified and sustainable planet, informed and animated by a lived sense of the common good, has never been so closely within our grasp. Having spent most of the course of human evolution reacting to threats, from predator and tyrant alike, it appears we are developing the aptitude and will to become more competent designers of our futures, to shift from a largely responsive disposition to a more proactive, intentional and creative mode.

Armed with profound new insights about how the world works, at all levels – from the human brain to the global climate – and how it might work better, it is not impossible today – current global ills notwithstanding – to imagine a future in which the Enlightenment's promise of universal freedom, equality and welfare is realized, with ecological health thrown in for good measure. From behavioral economics to positive psychology, from Google to the Grameen Bank, from ecosystem management to environmental justice, we possess the knowledge, tools, enterprises and finances to positively transform the human condition, and the ecological systems upon which we depend, at a scale never before seen, to move from where we are today to the better, more sustainable place most of us want to go.

Of course, between here and there lies the formidable bulwark of the status quo, a veritable fortress surrounding our entrenched mental models and political and economic institutions, and the possibility that the best laid plans will go awry. Maybe having already been set in motion, the forces of climate change will make my optimistic assessment moot, or perhaps the looming threat of terrorism of the kind that caused the date September 11 to be indelibly etched on our collective conscience will quash any hope of a sustainable future. No doubt there are many possible doomsday scenarios. That's the easy part.

The more challenging task, and by far the more

rewarding, is to sustain hope, to will to remain sanguine, notwithstanding contrary experience, just enough to continue to try to convince myself and others that a boldly green and just new world – a Republic of Trees – is ours to imagine, and to achieve. This book is about pointing the way, identifying some of the promising paths and likely pitfalls and increasing our level of awareness about what's possible – for people, place and the planet.

Part I : People

The visionary thinker John Thackara explains that, having designed ourselves into our problems, we can design ourselves out of them into a new reality. Social change begins with a rumor of this new reality, heard by someone paying attention, his ear to the ground, eager to prove the hearsay right. It starts with people – from a single actor to a mass movement – and builds from there

With so many different voices and points of view, so many different tolerances and appetites for civic life, it's often hard to imagine how we might create, let alone rally around, a shared vision of a new reality. After all, most Americans won't even cast a vote on Election Day, convinced that the game is over before it's begun. The idea that we would choose to devote considerable time and energy, to say nothing of an open mind, to envisioning an alternative, sustainable future, and then planning for and implementing it, seems far-fetched.

And often it is. Unskillfully orchestrated and yielding much more heat than light, important public discussions are frequently reduced to shouting matches among those brave few willing to show up. Meanwhile, the media, think tanks and politicians, with us, the public, their willing accomplices, have succeeded in creating an assemblage of air-tight echo-chambers, each resonating with the sounds of our own delusions and half-truths. If nothing else, we have proved adept at convincing ourselves of the rightness of our ideas and beliefs, even in the face of contrary compelling evidence or worse, the facts.

And yet, informed and inspired social decisionmaking can happen. And does. Over the past two decades, a growing movement for sustainable communities has emerged, in which public participation, community planning and other civic actions are the starting point for reimagining and reconstructing communities according to a new set of "sustainability" goals and benchmarks, grounded in a commitment to social justice, sound science and political accountability. Seniors and school children, new immigrants and natives, farmers and financiers – people from all walks of life are becoming engaged in the process of designing themselves out of their present predicaments and transforming negative patterns – in education, economic development, health care, land use and a host of other areas – into affirmative, positive ones. They are beginning to step out of their respective echo-chambers, question their own assumptions, listen to diverse viewpoints and envision new patterns and practices that integrate environmental concerns with issues such as jobs, schools, housing, transportation and energy.

Part I explores this novel kind of civic activity and the ups and downs associated with it. It covers a range of topics and examples in which people are confronted with a choice between business-as-usual or genuine change, between the default or something different. From backcountry skiing to baseball, immigration to innovation, Nantucket to nuclear energy, the writings in this chapter attempt to agitate, provoke and inspire new ways of looking at old problems and paradigms. They describe the challenges and solutions, and the individuals and ideas, changing how we govern and develop our places, and how we constructively engage with others in the process, to create vibrant, diverse and green communities on a shrinking, if not endangered, planet.

Clean Politics and Clean Environment Go Together

The Boston Globe
October 1999

As the 21st century nears, Massachusetts citizens have an opportunity to shape both their political and environmental future.

Thanks to the new state law allowing public financing of political campaigns and the proposed Sustainable Development Act, which was approved last week by the Legislature's Joint Natural Resources Committee, power could be vested in the people as never before to create the responsive politics and quality of life they desire.

The Sustainable Development Act would provide financial and technical support to local governments for regional planning aimed at achieving environmentally sound development across the state.

Though the development act and the campaign finance law were not designed as companions, they are flip sides of the same coin. Both rely on individual citizens and local communities to engage in the task of building better systems of democratic governance and better places to live. More important, these two goals are inextricably linked.

Environmental quality has everything to do with civic capacity; sustainable development hates political disaffection. Sustainable development must be understood as an ethical precept, a mandate to integrate into all development decisions a public concern for the protection of ecosystems and future generations.

In other words, sustainable development requires that we account for the environmental and social costs of development and avoid displacing those costs to another place or time. But without strong public involvement in political elections and local decision-making, critical sustainable development goals such as investment in mass transit, urban redevelopment, affordable housing and protection of wetlands and habitat are too easily abandoned in favor of private interests whose principal concern is making a profit and who for too long have exercised disproportionate power over the political system, underwriting campaigns and taking advantage of a political process too often lacking in public participation that can counteract their influence.

Weak political participation means that decision makers are not held accountable and that the narrow interests of a few can eclipse the broader public interest.

The lack of public engagement in the political process and local decision making leaves communities helpless to prevent environmental problems resulting from shortsighted development decisions and creates a downward spiral of democratic and environmental decay. The feeling of powerlessness many citizens express is reinforced by the environment in which they live, work, and play. Contaminated land, polluted rivers and streams, and other environmental problems undermine the physical integrity of communities and rob citizens of the sense of place that is at the heart of collective action.

Further, such problems inhibit the sense of stake and common purpose that encourages political participation and is the cornerstone of democracy.

Public participation and sustainable development go hand in hand. Citizen involvement, whether in political elections or public hearings, is the force that can temper the activities of the private sphere, establishing a healthy balance between the goals of public welfare and private gain.

Especially at the local level, where citizens and elected

officials are able to interact on an intimate and frequent basis and where environmental impacts are most visible, an engaged citizenry can ensure that decisions affecting their environment and quality of life are made with their substantial input and review. In the absence of such engagement, environmental harm invariably follows.

The public elections law opens the door to greater citizen involvement in local politics and civic life generally. Leveraging this new civic capacity, the Sustainable Development Act, now pending in the House, offers the promise of comprehensive local and regional planning that for the first time addresses the protection of ecosystems in their entirety and the welfare of future generations.

Taken together, the clean elections law and the Sustainable Development Act have set the stage for a merging of civic and environmental action, for a civic environmentalism, that is the essential precursor to sustainable development.

Massachusetts citizens should seize the moment and begin the process of creating a more democratic, more sustainable state.

Wish for Kings

National Public Radio "Living on Earth"
October 2000

As the presidential race enters its final, painstaking stages, many of us are still scratching our heads about who to vote for. Sure, a few, so-called "free-market" environmentalists will vote for George W. Bush. But for most of us the choice is between Democrat, Al Gore and Green Party candidate, Ralph Nader. Vice President Gore has been an outspoken environmentalist for nearly 20 years, and his book, Earth in the Balance, is a eloquent plea for the planet. Meanwhile, Nader is a hero to many, and brings a formidable record of reform and achievement to his candidacy. By most accounts, Nader really is the greenest candidate, from his austere personal habits – he doesn't even own a car – to his global environmental vision.

But, the dominance of the two major political parties makes the likelihood of a Nader win extremely low, which leaves environmentalists – especially in the predicted tight race – with something of a Hobson's choice: to vote for Nader is to vote for Bush; not to vote for Nader is to fail to make the most environmentally responsible decision. The situation doesn't allow for an easy solution, but does point to a deeper problem with our politics. Despite our more democratic, populist leanings, many of us still wish for kings. We claim to want the people to have the power, but look to individuals to save the day, to embody and enforce all our hopes and dreams for a better world, whether in a president or a pop star. We look to them for the authority and purposefulness we seem to lack in ourselves as a citizenry. But we have no Moses, or Gandhi, or Martin Luther King. Owing to the corruption of our political process by big money, we are foolish to expect an American President, produced by that selfsame process, to be able to enact the kind of far-reaching environmental reforms many of us want. At best, we can, and should, expect principled and accountable leadership, but not necessarily visionary leadership.

As poet Langston Hughes exhorted over half a century ago, it is we the people who must "redeem/The land, the mines, the plants, the rivers/The mountains and the endless plain/All, all the stretch of these great green states/And make America again!" It is we who must change our habits and practices, who must make better environmental decisions in our everyday lives. As the saying goes, when the people lead, the leaders will follow.

Lessons to Learn about Building Schools on Toxic Waste Sites

The Boston Globe
December 2000

The recent 11th-hour decision by Quincy Mayor James A. Sheets not to procced with the construction of a high school on a 24-acre toxic waste site is just the latest chapter in an unfolding textbook on urban land use and the growing demand for more and bigger public facilities like schools and libraries.

It is a chronicle of cities and towns across the country that are stretching their environmental limits, and of the desperate political acts of mayors, councilors, and parents braced by fear and few sound alternatives.

In Los Angeles earlier this year the board of education, fearing a parade of environmental horribles, voted to abandon a nearly completed high school after it was discovered that the oil field on which the school was built emitted dangerous levels of gases. The school was to educate 4,500 students from a largely low-income, Latino community long overdue for a new and larger facility.

Today, the building, which cost close to $200 million, is abandoned amid weeds and plastic sheathing, its fate still up in the air.

In Massachusetts, the city of Lowell is proposing to build a new middle school in the Acre neighborhood on one of the state's more notorious hazardous waste sites, a former coal gasification plant. After three years of planning and public meetings, the city determined that the eight-acre property was the only viable site for the much-needed school for the city's growing Cambodian and Latino school-age population.

Meanwhile, in Cambridge, the city council and community residents have been arguing for five years about where to put a new library, having outgrown the historic mid-Cambridge facility but with no room for expansion. The city originally proposed to build the new library on the two-acre park abutting the existing building, but that would eliminate the areas only significant green space. The battle rages on.

In Everett, a similar fight pitting four acres of parkland against a new high school was recently settled in favor of both, at least according to the mayor.

The high school will be built, but a new eight-acre park along the Malden River will also be developed to compensate for the lost open space. The problem is, that site, polluted industrial land owned by General Electric, might not be suitable for parkland.

What these examples show is that urban open space is in critically short supply and often polluted, and at a time when our need for new or expanded public facilities such as schools and libraries has never been greater.

Despite what appear to be no-win situations, however, some solutions are emerging that, though not perfect, appear to strike a balance between environmental quality and competing public goods.

In Lowell, for example, the city has engaged in a public participation process to inform and listen to community residents as environmental studies of the proposed school site proceed, should any surprises or new information about site conditions emerge.

As well, several city officials have expressed an interest in designing a new school that will not only create new open space for students and local residents, but incorporate green building techniques so that the school facility itself will teach the lesson of environmental responsibility, something like, from brownfield to green school. In Lowell, process, planning, and design are the three legs of the stool that, it is hoped, will support a new middle school.

While it appears that Quincy residents are fortunate to have other sites on which to build their school, many other cities aren't so lucky.

In a world of increasingly limited natural resources, especially in cities, we must discover in urban land use challenges opportunities for creativity and, most important, learning, attendant to legitimate fears of environmental disaster but also committed to the process, planning and design strategies Lowell is attempting.

Perhaps it should come as no surprise then that some of our most important environmental lessons are coming from our schools and libraries. Let's hope we're paying attention.

All Environmentalism Is Local

TomPaine.com
June 2001

A group of socially concerned artists recently decorated the windshields of hundreds of sport utility vehicles in the Boston area with mock traffi tickets. They were handing out citations of shame for drivers of what has become the premier symbol of Americans' in-your-face flouting of environmental responsibility.

The same thing's afoot in California. Stealthy citizens wielding anti-SUV bumper stickers are roving shopping mall parking lots, affixing the stickers to offending vehicles.

These creative strategies are being deployed in countless communities across the country. They reveal the frustration many Americans feel over the nation's inability to get over our infatuation with fossil fuels. And in a general sense, this local activism reveals an important emerging trend in environmentalism – away from traditional, inside-the-beltway approaches, and toward more creative, community-based actions.

What brought on this micro-environmentalism? Several factors.

First, people are responding to the failure of our federal environmental protection system to significantly change the way Americans – whether governments, firms, or individuals – consume.

Consider, for example, the Bush Administration's time-warped Energy Plan. Its unabashed call for full-scale development of fossil fuels, from coal to oil to natural gas, harkens back to the nineteenth century and the birth of the petroleum age. It's as if modern environmental laws, born of the oil spills, mining disasters, and soot-belching smoke stacks of the 1960s, didn't even exist.

Which brings us to the second reason we see action from the grassroots:

Modern environmentalism has been defined by high-powered national groups of lawyers and scientists headquartered in Washington, D.C., San Francisco, and New York. For thirty years, we've been committed to the notion that reform begins in the nation's capitol and spreads out from there.

The problem here, as the Bush Administration illustrates all too well, depending on who's in the White House, environmental reform is not necessarily a good thing. What one election cycle may give, another can just as easily take away.

Nonetheless, private foundations have overwhelmingly supported national environmental groups at the expense of local, grassroots efforts. Of the roughly half-billion dollars given each year to environmental organizations, seventy percent goes to fewer than fifty national groups. That leaves just thirty percent to be dispersed to some 20,000 local, largely volunteer efforts, notoriously short-staffed and with few resources.

What's the alternative? If the ratio of charitable monies were tilted even slightly in favor of the grassroots, local initiatives would flourish. It doesn't take much seed money to empower communities to fight the oil drilling, coal mining and power plant construction called for by the Bush plan. A little money would go a long way in unleashing communities' NIMBY – Not In My Back Yard – tendencies. Such local efforts could radically shift national energy policy, forcing a reconsideration of conservation measures and alternative technologies as energy priorities.

If the Bush Energy Plan offers environmentalists anything,

it is the unfortunate lesson that thirty years and billions of dollars spent doing battle in Washington, have yet to pay significant dividends or alter the terms of the debate. With more attention, and more philanthropic dollars directed to local and regional efforts, the situation can change.

Ticket by ticket, sticker by sticker, citizens are demonstrating that all environmentalism is local. It's time for the national groups and national funders to recognize this, and get more dollars flowing to the grassroots people who will make a difference.

Beyond Backyards and Bottom Lines

The Rutland Herald
October 2001

The conflict between environmentalism and development is almost as old as New England. In the early nineteenth century, Henry David Thoreau, retreating to the woods near Walden Pond, lamented that "For one that comes with a pencil to sketch or sing, a thousand come with an ax or rifle." Later in the century, the Vermonter George Perkins Marsh, the man responsible for reforesting Woodstock after decades of clear-cutting, admonished "Man has too long forgotten that the earth was given to him for usufruct alone, not for consumption, still less for profligate waste."

Today, not much has changed. From the forests of the Pacific Northwest to the ski resorts of the Rocky Mountains to the Northeastern suburbs, battles are raging between those bent on saving the environment and those trying to develop it. They have become a truism of American life and a staple of local headlines. Regrettably, in Vermont, the situation is no different. Recent proposals to build a big-box hardware store, a natural gas pipeline, and a quarry, to name a prominent few, have each met with formidable resistance, dividing individuals and communities across the build/no-build chasm.

But these controversies, despite the rhetoric, are not really about environmental protection or economic development. At bottom, they are about the responsibilities of citizenship, individual and corporate, and what it means to live in the world beyond the bounds of one's own backyard or bottom line. To be sure, the environment versus development debate posits a false choice, a specious dualism that has long gone unchallenged. Development is, after all, a natural process. Ecosystems, any good scientist or environmental historian will tell you, are not static but grow and change over time. Like human economies, natural systems move through cycles of growth and decline, produce goods and services (think of Vermont's forests, manufacturing all manner of useful commodities like lumber and maple syrup while providing invaluable services such as filtering air pollutants and stabilizing soils that would otherwise erode away), and even generate waste (observe the colorful carpet of leaves, autumn's detritus, now covering the forest floor).

Further, thanks to advances in environmental design, planning and engineering, development doesn't have to come at the expense of environmental quality. Quite the contrary. In Burlington's Intervale section, for example, city planners, environmentalists, and businesses are building an "eco-industrial park." Part of a larger trend called sustainable development, these innovative facilities incorporate production practices and design features that mimic the reuse, recycling and replenishing functions of natural systems, like forests or wetlands. By converting one firm's waste into another's energy, using non-toxic and recycled materials, and employing energy-efficient technologies, eco-industrial development simultaneously protects the environment while providing economic benefits like jobs and taxes.

The environment versus development debate masks the real problem: most Americans are neither prepared nor willing to engage with open minds and a public spirit in discussions about difficult policy decisions – whether environmental protection, civil rights, affordable housing, health care, or any number of issues – whose consequences, both positive and negative, cut across economic, social and political interests. Long a culture that celebrates the individual over the community, the corporation over the commonwealth, we have a weak tradition of public dialogue, of deliberative democracy. Additionally, Americans have shown an aversion to participation in public affairs. Only fifty per cent vote in public elections, the lowest rate of any non-compulsory democracy, while less than ten per cent bother to show up at community meetings. As the political scientist Robert Putnam has noted, the nation's social capital – the community networks, norms and trust that facilitate cooperation among groups for mutual benefit – is waning, inhibiting our ability, as he puts it, to develop the "I" into "We."

"Democracy," the late Texas congresswoman Barbara Jordan argued, "cannot be saved by supermen, but only by the unswerving devotion of millions of middle men." To move beyond the environment versus development debate requires the commitment of ordinary citizens, connected by their place, economy, and social bonds, to respectful and informed dialogue about the decisions that fundamentally affect their lives and express what they stand for as communities. In most places, this commitment is sorely lacking.

But if any place has the ability to save democracy, it is Vermont. In its robust town meeting tradition, progressive policies on a host of important and controversial social issues, and abiding commitment to rural culture and environmental quality, Vermont has shown a unique capacity for civic discourse and social problem-solving. It is thus no accident that creative development strategies like Burlington's eco-park or Bennington's and Rutland's downtown-friendly Wal-Mart have been pioneered in Vermont. But projects like these are few, and most are still in their infancy. The challenge in Vermont and across the land is not simply to replicate these efforts and take them to scale, but devise new ones, ever mindful that we should not let the perfect become the enemy of the good.

Out of the ashes of September's terrorist attacks has arisen an unprecedented opportunity for citizens to come together around shared interests and goals. If this is to be more than simply superficial gestures of solidarity, we must work to enact in our day-to-day practices the good faith, openness to new ideas, and concern for the common good that are the hallmarks of democratic citizenship. In the Green Mountain State, where ecology, economy, and culture are so closely aligned, these virtues should come naturally.

The Democracy of the Backcountry

The Rutland Herald
February 2002

The Bush administration's recent action overturning the Clinton-proposed ban on snowmobiles in Yellowstone and Grand Teton National Parks has got me rethinking a 4-year old vow. My wife Sally was six months pregnant with our first child at the time and, being the avid backcountry skiers that we are, we thought nothing of it one mid-morning in early January when we headed into the wilderness behind Stratton Mountain to make fresh tracks in 10 inches of powder. Trouble was, as we skied across Stratton Pond about half-way through our 8 mile route, Sally's legs began to fatigue to the point of failure. We didn't realize that with the later stages of pregnancy comes a softening of the cartilage, not to mention less energy in reserve. We had no choice. We had to stop. It was cold and the sky was darkening.

I had traveled the area enough to know two things that bore on our predicament. First, we rarely saw other skiers on the trail, so we couldn't rely on anyone skiing by. Second, about a mile ahead of us was an old logging road that was a favorite among snowmobilers. I skied ahead to look for help, leaving Sally with some food and water. It wasn't long before a small caravan of snowmobilers heeded my signal and stopped to see what was up. Without a second thought, they agreed to help and waited patiently while I went to retrieve my wife. An hour later we were back at the trailhead, as grateful as we were unnerved.

For years before this incident, I had held snowmobilers in mild contempt. For backcountry skiers and snowshoers, snowmobiles are an annoying fact of life, like mosquitoes but much louder and with a lingering odor that can make a wilderness path smell like an interstate. Of course, because of the inherent danger of snowmobiling, most riders wear large, bulbous helmets with thick visors and lots of padding. The result is they can neither hear nor smell their own machines. But that's precisely what's so odd about snowmobiling, more a motorized activity than a sport: Riders can travel over vast distances within a matter of hours, an amount that would require a skier or snowshoer several days, and yet, owing to their equipment, they really can't experience the scenery, the backcountry, at all, save for when they've stopped, turned off their engines and taken off their helmets.

But that January day, safe and warm in our parked car, I vowed never to say another nasty word about snowmobiles and the folks who ride them, all winter's day and night, throughout Vermont's backcountry and farm fields.

Now, however, the Bush administration's proposal has me rankled to the point of abandoning my vow. For years, the Department of Interior has solicited public comment on the question of snowmobiles in the national parks and the public has consistently favored a ban, pointing to the machine's noxious emissions and throaty drone. Pollution at the West Entrance to Yellowstone, where at daybreak over a thousand snowmobiles may be assembled, has gotten so bad that the National Park Service has had to pump fresh air into the park rangers booths and provide the rangers with respirators. The result is that many of our parks and backcountry areas have been transformed into snow-covered speedways, much closer to a NASCAR event than any wilderness experience.

The snowmobile industry, who in June 2001 negotiated a procedural settlement with the Bush administration that required the Department of Interior to consider alternatives allowing for snowmobile access to the parks, is a force to be reckoned with, not only in Washington but much closer to home. It's no accident that when my wife and I got stranded in the woods are best hope for rescue lay with snowmobilers and not skiers. To borrow a line from the motorcycle set, snowmobilers are everywhere. Skiers, conversely, are scarce. In Vermont, the state snowmobile association has 33,000 members. The skiing counterpart, the Catamount Trail Association, of which I'm a member, has a mere 1500. That's 22 snowmobilers for every one skier. No wonder the industry is so powerful: it's got the bodies and they're mobilized.

Wrapped up in my disdain for snowmobiles is a grudging admiration for the people who ride them. I mean, these folks are actually out there enjoying the backcountry, those roughly 300,000 million acres of public lands across the U.S. Meanwhile, we skiers and snowshoers remain a fragile, self-righteous few, no match for the lobbying prowess, not to mention horsepower, of the snowmobilers. It's disheartening to see just how few Americans, without the use of motorized vehicles, use the backcounty, no matter what the season.

And therein lies the rub. Until there are more skiers and snowshoers using our public lands and organizing themselves into a formidable political force, the mechanics of democracy will continue to work against us. So skiers and snowshoers, unite, take up your gear, and head for the hills. There's still plenty of room.

Civic By Nature

Urban Ecology Magazine
Spring 2002

By nature, cities are tough places, the architectural elegance of the built form masking the sometimes brutish, always stressful conditions that attend urban living. Even today, in the U.S., while urban centers are experiencing a revival after decades of decline, cities remain challenging places to live and raise a family due to the oft-cited parade of urban problems: bad schools, expensive housing, crime, and poor public services. Unfortunately, smart growth and redevelopment efforts that seek to reverse these conditions often ignore, or even undermine, something just as important to urban revitalization: environmental quality.

It's not just that people crave spacious parks and green spaces for recreation and repose. Nor that environmental assets like mature street trees provide significant economic value, not to mention health benefits, to cities. These are truisms. More fundamental than these is the carrying capacity of urban ecosystems: the ability of the urban environment to sustain diverse living systems over time at a reasonable quality. In the light of cities' improved image, we face an unnerving paradox today. The same forces responsible for revitalizing cities run the risk of inundating them with more physical and economic growth than natural systems can handle. The potential consequences are dire: frequent severe flooding from lack of drainage; extreme heat islands due to dark surfaces like black-topped streets and rooftops; every last vestige of green space swallowed up by development; the insidious spread of invasive species; persistent air and water pollution from myriad point and non-point sources. These impacts also entail serious physical and psychological health risks, less easily quantifiable but equally pernicious. In too many urban neighborhoods, we have created what the writer David Quammen calls a "planet of weeds," places so ecologically bankrupt that only cockroaches, kudzu and crows can survive. So how do we elevate urban ecology – whether street trees or floodplains, invasive species or air pollution – to a more prominent place in urban policy and planning? I believe it must begin with people, not abstractions like government or the private market. As the old saying goes, folkways change stateways, not the other way around. Landlords and homeowners are a good place to start because the residential footprint in most cities is so expansive, presenting a powerful (albeit diffuse) leverage point for restoring environmental quality to built-out urban communities.

With little effort and investment, landlords and homeowners can effect significant ecological improvements. They can demolish their asphalt driveways and parking lots and replace them with a quality pervious material like stone or gravel, providing instant increased drainage. Where backyard soils have been contaminated due to lead paint or other toxic releases, clean compost can be trucked in for just a few dollars a cubic foot to cap the contamination and provide a base for planting native plants. And by simply monitoring the health of trees and vegetation on public sidewalks and streets, and contacting public works officials when maintenance is necessary, all city residents can directly influence the quality of public green space. These investments in labor and materials are quickly off-set by increased property values, not to mention more useable, enjoyable outdoor space.

While this kind of civic approach to ecological restoration cannot solve every urban environmental problem, it's a practical step forward that doesn't require a major shift in policy or market practices, the lack of which can too easily become an excuse for inaction. What this approach does require is a commitment to one's own place and community that is the necessary precondition to any voluntary civic act and, in turn, to broader social change. In the aggregate, the individual actions of environmentally aware citizens can have profound consequences for both policymaking and market institutions, not to mention backyard environmental quality.

Small steps can be beautiful, to paraphrase E.F. Schumacher. As a society that celebrates the big and the brash, whether in politics or commerce, we have a dangerous tendency to overlook the humble, what Daniel Kemmis calls "the simple, homely practices which are the last best hope for revival of genuine public life" and, I believe, environmental protection. Lacking any other kind of dependable environmental leadership, we simply don't have the luxury of waiting for someone, or something, beyond ourselves and our communities to fix our problems. All we have is ourselves, and our street trees. We must work to keep it that way.

Fraud and Forests

TomPaine.com
November 2002

Perhaps it's that I live and work in the Boston area, New England's metropolis awash, like every other major U.S. city, in the culture of corporate capitalism and global commerce, but I'm feeling overwhelmed lately. The on-going accounts of shady schemes and glaring greed among many of the nation's leading business executives, the same ones so excessively hyped up by the mainstream media only a few short years ago, are having a corrosive psychic effect, leaving me both stupefied and with a deep sense of ethical longing – for a less corrupt, less venal, less fraudulent culture.

Of course, today's corporate scandals are nothing new. Following every economic boom in American history have come revelations of the debauchery and decadence that at once fueled the boom and ultimately brought down many of its principals, not to mention the savings and spirits of countless ordinary citizens. But the current economic – no, cultural – crisis is different. In an age when Americans' social and physical environments have become so standardized, so denatured, thanks largely to the relentless rush to profitability and scale – whether by WorldCom or Wal-Mart, Global Crossing or Gap, Dynegy or Disney – that defines modern day capitalism and is at the root of the crisis, many of us were already suffering from corporate fatigue. The recent scandals have put us on sick leave.

The result is a wrenching hunger for authenticity – for the real versus the artificial, the organic versus the processed, the homespun versus the mass-produced. This pent-up desire underlies much of Americans' anxiety at the start of the twenty-first century. For me, a good dose of relief derives from New England's forests.

From Thoreau and Muir to Marsh and Burroughs to Leopold and Carson, for at least two centuries Americans have sought out hope and spiritual renewal in untamed landscapes. Steeped in this tradition, though wary of its tendency to over-romanticize wilderness, I escape to the woods to experience nature's unvarnished, unforgiving side, what Ezra Pound called "the eternal moods of the bleak wind. . . the strong loneliness of sunless cliffs." I come to test my skills, not just the kind I learned as a teenager at the National Outdoor Leadership School, where I spent five hard weeks adrift in Wyoming's Wind River mountains, but the building blocks of a responsible, ethical life: hard work, preparation, endurance, awareness, and self-knowledge.

I spend a lot of time exploring the rugged terrain of southern Vermont's White Rocks National Recreation Area, roughly 36,000 acres in the Green Mountain National Forest between Mt. Tabor, Wallingford, and Weston. On foot, skis, or snowshoes, and with topo maps at hand, I like to venture off piste, using overgrown roads and natural features as my guide. The experience is always new, and always challenging: the endless steep and rocky slopes, darkened in summer by a thick canopy of trees; the stream beds cascading every which way; the beaver ponds and meadows, soggy swaths of open space hinged to the forest's edge. At lower elevations, primitive stonewalls and logging roads languish in the undergrowth. Higher up, the woods get steeper and denser until the alpine zone, where, surrounded only by sedges, dwarf conifers and bare rock, you are naked to the elements. It's a far cry from the local park or nature center. You learn quickly that in these parts you can't hoodwink nature, can't sell her a bill of goods. She will find you out, then expose you to the wind.

I come to the forest not only to challenge myself, but to discover the forest's myriad rewards: moose tracks in the mud, the flesh-colored leaves of a beech tree fluttering in a February wind, the sweet smell of balsam, the silhouette of a barred owl at dusk. Nature's unmediated presence is a great moral touchstone, a reminder of both the awesome power and sublime grandeur that exist outside human intervention while demanding of us discipline, respect, and, above all, humility. These are virtues absent from so much of corporate America and the culture at large. These are the hardscrabble virtues the forest teaches us.

Over a decade ago, in the aftermath of the nation's last boom-bust cycle, the notorious corporate raider Charles Hurwitz, eager to sell off some of his assets to pay down mountainous debts, proposed clear-cutting one of northern California's last great stands of ancient redwoods, the 4500-acre Headwaters Forest, owned in part by his company, Pacific Lumber. Of course, Hurwitz couldn't tell the difference between a redwood and a red maple. Based in Houston, Texas, his company, Maxxam, is in business solely to buy companies, any companies, and then unload them quickly, in the process liquidating their assets to maximize profits. Thanks to the mass opposition of outraged citizens, of tree-huggers, Hurwitz's plans have so far been thwarted, though the fate of the forest is still undecided. Nonetheless, the story stands as a parable for today's corporate behavior. Forests may be threatened, but the principles they embody, and the passion they inspire, can prevail, like pioneer trees reclaiming old fields.

In the end, corporate responsibility is just another name for the cardinal environmental ethics: tread lightly, be humble, respect all living things, and consider the collective before the individual. From my office in the city, I can hear the beech leaves rustling, along the ridge, off the trail leading to the beaver meadows. The forest speaks. Will corporate America listen?

Earth Day

Connecticut College Keynote Address
April 2003

Thanks to the event organizers, the Mitchell Trust, Preserve East Lyme, the Connecticut College Arboretum, and the Connecticut College Students Against Violence to the Environment, and especially Randall Lucas, for inviting me to be with you tonight. It's a pleasure to be here, at the mouth of the mighty Thames, in this happily forgotten corner of New England (save, I should add, for a few notable casinos nearby).

Now I first got to know your college when I was in high school in Connecticut and ventured to write a book about some of the state's oldest and most interesting trees, only to find out that your arboretum, and its director Glenn Dreyer, had beaten me to it, with their excellent volumes on the state's Notable Trees. This resource later came in quite handy when I discovered that my in-laws, who live in nearby Lyme, Connecticut, on the banks of the Connecticut River, hosted on their property one of the most magnificent sugar maples I've ever seen, which I was convinced was among the oldest and largest in the state. I encouraged them to give Glenn a call to find out and wouldn't you know it, his assessment determined it was Connecticut's third largest sugar maple on record.

So you see I'm a tree hugger by nature, and a fan of your college as a result. How could I not be, with a campus that doubles as an arboretum. Talk about green campuses!

Beyond my tree-hugger credentials, I'm also someone who's passionate about the land – land in the literal and metaphorical sense – land as nature, land as people, a nation-state, a culture. To me, landscape and democracy, environment and community, are one. In reading the landscape, we read about ourselves, whether in cities or countryside. Trouble is, it's often not a pretty picture, what with the waste dumps, the polluted waterways (40 percent unfishable and unswimmable), the paved over wetlands (half of the original wetlands gone since 1790), the strip malls and cookie-cutter subdivisions, the abandoned brownfield sites (almost 600,000, enough land area to better Los Angeles county). What a contrast to this arboretum-campus, and so many other universities across the country, as pristine in their design and development as any wilderness area.

Which brings us to this Earth Day. Tonight, I want to talk to you about the importance of the university, and more to the point, you, its students – in breaking down barriers – institutional, intellectual, spatial – and becoming engaged in the life and struggles of the places and people around you, a topic not unfamiliar to Connecticut College, which has been a pioneer in building bridges between the college and its community, in this case the city of New London. Engagement and place, democracy and landscape, this, for me, is what environmentalism's all about.

And it really started in college. I went to Brown University in Providence, Rhode Island, just up the interstate. Though I was a history concentrator, I spent much of my time at the Urban Environmental Laboratory, a unique program that housed the environmental studies department and, more importantly, served as the gateway for students interested in doing community service work and exploring the places and people of Providence beyond the walls of the unblighted Brown campus.

I designed and led urban environmental programs for kids from the city's hardscrabble southside neighborhood, exploring Providence's street trees, its then-hidden river, the Providence (since opened up as part of the city's revitalization in the early 1990s), its many hills and parks, its built landscape.

These experiences, though extracurricular, resonated powerfully with me and helped to shape not just my career aspirations, but my basic world view and social principles. Over the course of my college career, I became not just a committed environmentalist, but a critical one. I realized, as so many others have, that environmentalism has not well served many people and many places. Communities of color, urban communities, for example. They've been left out, marginalized, in favor of greener, or more precisely, whiter pastures.

At the same time, I also came to realize that our universities have too often ignored the very communities in which they reside; that, like environmentalism, these institutions have neglected too many people and places, not coincidentally the same ones left behind by environmentalists. It's no accident that town versus gown looks an awful lot like city folk versus tree-huggers.

My college experiences were in this way transformative. They gave me a rigorous framework, both intellectual and practical, with which to understand and explain my calling as an environmentalist and social entrepreneur, someone committed to changing the ways things are, to helping build communities more in balance with the natural systems that ultimately make those communities function.

You see, for the past decade I've worked as an attorney and educator on behalf of people and places in this country, and particularly New England, left behind by our traditional environmental protection system and environmentalism itself. My work in the field and the classroom is based on the idea that the environment is everybody's business, no matter where we live or who we are. It is also grounded in the notion that our environment, our places, are as much something we construct and shape as they are something we experience. Again, we and our environment constitute eachother, biologically and culturally. Land as nature, land as people.

Now, this work is daunting, often vexing. Consider that about three out of four Americans claim to be environmentalists, regardless of the costs of environmental protection programs. Yet, when it comes to our consumer choices, we belie this fact, buying bigger cars and bigger houses than anyone else on the planet and voting into office politicians whose environmental credentials are as weak as they're aversion to progressive social policy is strong. Especially today, with the Bush Administration's frontal assault on environmental policy, we seem to have stepped back in time to the late nineteenth century, when all that mattered was our ability to extract oil and other resources with abandon.

Despite this, and you can call me crazy, I have come to believe there is no better, more exciting time to be a young environmentalist than today. I can say this because as students, you have at your disposal access to knowledge, ideas, technologies, and practices that were simply not available just a generation ago. The rise of the sustainability movement, of environmental justice, of regionalism and smart growth, of green design, of civic environmentalism, of adaptive management, of green business, of industrial ecology: these are several of the many emerging, dare I say growing, trends that signal a pivotal and promising shift in the way we live on the planet and with eachother, one more in tune with the way natural systems work and more sensitive to the basic requirements of democratic community, namely, that ordinary folks, not just the experts, the industrialists, and the politicians, who for too long have dominated the playing field, should be engaged in the decisionmaking over matters that fundamentally affect the quality of their lives.

But now the tough part, again. For just as we have developed new ways of solving old problems, so too have we come to a new understanding of just how urgent, and how complicated, our environmental problems are. We no longer have the luxury of simply targeting for protection individual wildlife species like spotted owls or snail darters, or buying up small islands of pristine land amidst oceans of sprawl, or controlling pollutants one by one.

Thanks to a revived practice of systems thinking, hard-earned lessons from the sciences about such realities as global climate change, ozone transport, and endocrine disruption, and the everyday experiences of a growing number of concerned citizens, we now realize that to protect individual species and individual places means we have to protect entire ecosystems, entire landscapes, entire watersheds; that to really solve pollution problems it's not enough simply to deal with them individually from easily controlled sources like smokestacks but instead we must look at the entire life cycle of pollutants, from cradle to cradle, to ensure that we're not playing what's been for the past 30 years a dangerous shell game: remove some quantity of air pollutant X from a smoke stack in place A and transfer it to a landfill in place B where it then becomes someone else's soil pollution problem at some other time. This is what the economist's call a negative externality and what I call plain short-sightedness, irresponsibility.

And we have come to realize that to be effective, to match the scale and complexity of the challenge, environmentalists must diversify themselves and their tools. We must move beyond the demographics of affluent white suburbanites, beyond the tools of law and litigation, to deepen and expand our capacity to effect the change we claim to seek.

But this is not all. In the light of the on-going war in Iraq and its precursor events, we have again been reminded of just how tightly environmental issues are woven into the fabric of our economic and political lives. Many of us who can recall the war against Iraq just over a decade ago see in the current crisis not only the politics of the Middle East or terrorism, not merely America's foreign policy challenges or the burden of our superpower status, but a much simpler, more banal theme: our pathologic dependence on oil to power not only our economy, but our national self-image. Oil is what distinguishes Iraq from Bosnia, from East Timor, from Somalia, from Rwanda; nothing more, nothing less. Today, more than we did even just 12 years ago, we know how bad the consequences of this dependence, this addiction, can be.

This is the burden of knowledge, the burden of understanding. It raises the bar of responsibility and complexity for those courageous enough to act on it.

Which is what I want to urge each of you to do today, to act, to be bold, to step up to this challenge, as no doubt many of you have already begun to do. "We live," the lawyer-poet Wallace Stevens, who also happened to be Hartford insurance executive, wrote, "in an old chaos of the sun." It is indeed a messy, chaotic world, always was. But even here, in Stevens's lyrical wisdom, is an environmental metaphor and glimmer of hope: the sun, our greatest renewable resource, a substitute, for oil and all its pathologies.

In whatever bright light you can find amidst the chaos, and it is there, I want to urge you smart Connecticut College activists to defy the tendency to feel overwhelmed and desperate in these times and instead to allow yourselves to find hope in the opportunities for change – social, political, environmental – however modest or ephemeral they might seem, to pursue with gusto those things that really matter. This is the gift of our progress in understanding the ways of ecosystems. It is also the mandate issued by the current war.

But for this you must be patient, prepared for the long-haul, for the work of building sustainable communities, for building a society in greater harmony with itself and nature, is not only about solving a complex set of problems, but understanding that the roots of these problems extend 300 years deep into the soil of the American system – our preference for profits and property rights above collective concerns, out of balance, out of step with our better selves and aspirations. They will not be reformed over night, not even in a decade or two. Perhaps a century, maybe more.

Just as the time is ripe for change, it is even riper for change agents, for change makers, you who are idealistic enough to take the leap, but smart enough to know how, nurtured in a fine liberal arts college, one of the last vestiges of idealism and public values we have.

The rewards of this work are deeply personal, ineffable. To the extent that each of you finds yourself wondering each day at nature's mysteries and beauty – the undulating hills of oak and hemlock meandering to the banks of the Thames, a college steeple rising to meet the sound at sunset, that old sugar maple in a long abandoned field – then act, work to protect and celebrate those things that matter most. For those of you who find yourselves called to a career that defies a simple job description, I say go for it.

And on that note, let me leave you with these lines from another great American voice, Adrienne Rich, the Berkeley poet, who writes of this difficult world, "It will not be simple, it will take all your breath, it will become your will." Yes, it will take all your breath.

Good luck, go forth, change the world. It's never too late.

Too Much 'Island Thinking' on Nantucket

The Boston Globe
August 2003

I have fond memories of summers on Nantucket,
my father reading *Moby-Dick* to me and my sister as we
searched across Nantucket Bay for the great white whale
from the porch of the Wauwinet beach house we rented
every August. The island was a different place back then,
quiet and provincial, a cobblestoned community of hardy
year-rounders and the preppy summer set attracted to the
island's proud maritime past and pristine setting. Despite
these memories, I've come to think twice about Nantucket
after several visits this summer. Three controversies speak to
what I call an "island" mentality that defies the very idea of
the Commonwealth of which Nantucket is a part. This way
of thinking asserts the primacy of the individual above the
collective without exception. Island thinking is the opposite
of the Commonwealth idea, which holds that as citizens
we must think not only about ourselves but others, must
recognize that our fates are entwined.

The first controversy involves affordable housing. With
only 2.5 percent of the island's housing stock qualifying as
affordable – a quarter of the state minimum standard – and
the average price of a Nantucket home hovering around $1
million, the need for affordable housing on the island could
not be greater. My brother-in-law, an elementary school
principal, interviewed for a job on Nantucket a few years
ago only to withdraw his candidacy after reviewing the real
estate options. With 40 percent of the island's land protected
from development, the simple rules of supply and demand
have made Nantucket one of the nation's most exclusive
communities.

Further, despite a string of recent proposals to build more affordable housing, resistance is visceral and effective. Millionaire summer residents, their lawyers at the ready, decry proposal after proposal as a scandalous, unsightly assault on the island's precious green spaces. These litigious islanders have made not-in-my-backyard an elite sport, like polo, reserved for those with money to spend and a nose for a dirty fight. Not surprising, little progress has been made in building affordable units in the last decade. Nantucket continues to rank at the bottom among Massachusetts cities and towns.

Raging alongside the affordable housing row is the season's true cause celebre, the fight against a proposal by Cape Wind to build 130 wind turbines 14 miles off Nantucket on Horseshoe Shoal. The project would provide on average three-quarters of the energy needs of Nantucket, Martha's Vineyard, and Cape Cod and is the most significant renewable energy project ever proposed in New England. It's a private-sector response to the growing need for locally produced power brought about by global climate change, a deregulated utility industry, and the national security risks associated with Middle East oil.

Notwithstanding minimal aesthetic and environmental impacts and the intense scrutiny of 17 state and federal agencies, the project's opponents, many of whom reside on Nantucket, are unbending in their belief that the wind farm will forever "industrialize" the region, undermining its fragile ecosystems and maritime appeal. With the likes of Walter Cronkite, the Kennedy family, big-name CEOs, and dozens of other high-powered landowners digging in their heels, the antiwind forces, like their counterparts battling affordable housing, have time and money on their side.

SUVs round out the trinity of island controversies. Maligned by locals and visitors alike because of their size and numbers, the SUV is perhaps the most fitting and menacing symbol of the island mentality. Where once station wagons and rust-covered Jeeps ruled, the SUVs that now dominate the island are too wide for its 18th-century streets and single-lane secondary roads, too tall for the tree-lined curbsides of town, and too aggressive for its proverbially quaint setting. In their great girth and towering stance, supersized rigs that lumber up and down the island's roads and beaches stand for one thing only: the power of me.

The Nantucket I knew as a child is gone. It went the way of the rusty Jeeps. And that's OK. Today's Nantucket is more diverse and more dynamic than yesterday's, with its cosmopolitan feel, flourishing arts community, rising immigrant population, and even a local vodka distiller.

But what these three struggles suggest is that today's Nantucket is also too much of an island, not enough of a Commonwealth. There needs to be greater balance – more affordable housing, more wind turbines, fewer SUVs.

This isn't so much a function of rulemaking or regulation as it is of mind-set. The Commonwealth idea needs to be learned and lived by all Nantucketers – year-round and summer, resident and visitor, wealthy and low-income – so that the interests of the individual and the collective can be better aligned.

Perhaps this will prove as difficult a quest as the hunt for the great white whale. But if I learned nothing else from my father's readings those quiet summer evenings overlooking the bay, it's that in Ahab's mad pursuit was also a dream of righting wrongs. We may never take the whale, but I hope at least we try.

The Skye Boat Song: Lessons from Art and Youth

New Canaan Country School Alumni Award Lecture
February 2004

First, let me say a heart-felt thanks to Tim Bazemore, Jane Isaacs, and the Alumni Council for this special honor. Besides the award itself, this occasion has been especially gratifying because it's reconnected me to what has seemed until now a distant past. Looking at the eager faces of the students and seeing old friends, I'm reminded that the past is present; it is here and now.

In fact, looking out on this assembly, I can see myself as a small boy, curly blond hair (you might have noticed a slightly different hue), clutching a heavy, red song book. It's music class. We're gathered – fourth, fifth and sixth graders – all together in the old assembly hall, just across the way. Mr. Huwiler, the wry, bespeckled music director famous for flinging his glasses off one ear at the slightest hint of a wrong note, has just called on me, a nervous fourth-grader with a girl's soprano voice, cheeks turning red, to sing a verse of the English sea shanty, the Skye Boat Song. The song tells of the escape of Bonnie Prince Charles to the Isle of Skye in 1746, having suffered a defeat in battle to the Duke of Cumberland:

> Speed bonnie boat, like a bird on the wing
> Onward, the sailors cry
> Carry the lad that's born to be king
> Over the sea to Skye.

I still sing this hymn often, a man of 39, no longer a high-pitched soprano but a throatier tenor. I recall this moment in Mr. Huwiler's music class, under his often uncomfortable spotlight – after all, most 4th grade boys want to be singled out on the athletic field, not in music class (gosh, what would the girls think?) – I recall this because I believe it speaks to something very powerful about the Country School, this place of learning and playing and singing bounded only by old maple trees, stone walls, and the imagination of a child looking out from the soccer field, as I often did, to the verdant ridgelines off to the east, thinking of mountains, and sunshine, and far-off places, and a future I could not even comprehend.

Those moments in Mr. Huwiler's music class bring to mind two thoughts about your Country School experience I'd like to share with you today. These reflections, I think, underscore the fact, as I suggested earlier, that what's past is present, not merely prologue, that the enriching experiences and boundless vistas of your youth can, and indeed should, continue to be with you as you grow and venture out into the wider world.

The first reflection has to do with art, with creativity, with the simple act of making and doing something new and different even if it's embarrassing or uncomfortable because it's revealing. You see, like most boys, I really only wanted to be an athlete when I was your age. Soccer, hockey, lacrosse, skiing: these were the things that, I thought, most mattered in life. Man, did I spend a lot of time worrying about sports, thinking about them, looking forward to my father taking me to what was then the mecca of all sporting goods stores, Bob's Sports, to get that new pair of sneakers or new hockey stick, eagerly awaiting the first pond skating, the first snowfall for skiing.

Now don't get me wrong, athletics and physical activity are a wonderful thing, a central part of living a good and balanced life. This is why the esteemed Greek academies of ancient times all had Gymnasiums, places to exercise the Body. The Greeks believed, rightly, that a sound Body and sound Mind go hand in hand.

My sports addiction continues to this day. Just ask my wife Sally. She'll tell you, perhaps with fists clenched, that I'm just another sports guy, drawn to anything with a ball or stick that appears on the television screen. My son Shepard seems to be picking up the habit.

But what Mr. Huwiler taught me was that part of growing, of enriching one's life, is cultivating a variety of talents, art alongside athletics. I was embarrassed to sing the Skye Boat Song in front of my peers because I believed, like every other kid in the room, that boys, especially boys with high voices, should be soccer players, not singers. That was what my peer group, and my society, told me. But Mr. Huwiler, himself a musician of course, knew better. Like all great teachers, he saw in me a love for music that I didn't acknowledge or understand at the time, but that came, invariably, from my own mother and growing up in a household where Stephen Sondheim and Stevie Wonder were the soundtrack to my youth.

And you know what, I never looked back. From that point on, starting in fourth grade, I became a singer and a music lover. I started playing piano and guitar, launched a rock band in high school, performed in coffee houses in college and graduate school, and still sing and play guitar to this day, perhaps to the chagrin of my neighbors in Cambridge, Massachusetts where I live, but I play nonetheless. Despite my career as an environmental lawyer and professor, where music and other artistic expression too often seem out of place, I've always found room for music. It's provided some of my most cherished and happy moments. Thanks to Mr. Huwiler, the Skye Boat Song is alive, today, in this room and in me, just as it was three decades ago.

So I want to urge you to discover your own version of the Skye Boat Song as you learn and nurture new talents here at the Country School. Maybe it's painting, or woodworking, or violin, or poetry; maybe it's dance or pottery; maybe it's simply appreciating these things, wondering at them, learning about them. Let your teachers help you discover what you might be afraid or unaware of in yourself; let your hidden talents – the gifts that your peers and even your parents might scoff at – be revealed and nurtured so that as you grow, they might continue to provide and sustain you. After all, your body will inevitably wither, will weaken with age and wear. Your days on the playing field are numbered. But art and your passion for it, these things you take with you in your heart and mind. They transcend the body. They are your soul.

Which brings me to my other thought regarding Mr. Huwiler's music class. Now, on occasions like these it's customary for me, the speaker, to offer up the vast wisdom of my years, in my case all 39 of them, to you, the eager and impressionable young people convened to hear a guy you've never seen before nor likely will ever see again. And perhaps the first part of my talk affirms this tradition. But the second part debunks it.

You see, if my parable is in part about the virtues of art and cultivating diverse talents in your youth, it's also about the importance of youthful spirit in an all-too-adult world, it's about the subversive, the dangerous notion that adults – despite their age, their suits and ties, their authority – don't have all the answers, all the lessons, all the wisdom to impart, including me.

I like to think that each time I sing "speed bonnie boat" I'm reminding myself that I'm still young at heart, still willing to try new things, to explore new ground, however timid, uncomfortable, or unsure I might feel. As adults, we kid ourselves (pun intended) into believing we have the answers, that there's nothing new under the sun, that, as the saying goes, "we've been there and done that."

But you know what, the young person in me knows better. In a world where war and poverty, discrimination, greed and avarice, where fanaticism and environmental degradation persist, it's fair to say that we adults – the same ones who run our governments, our corporations, and other powerful institutions – we adults often know less than we think we know, but are usually reluctant to admit it. As adults, we tend to get stuck in our ways, our habits, our ideologies. The world is the way it is, we say, because it's the way it is. This is the adults' insidious tautology, our flawed circular reasoning. I know, I'm an adult. There's an aphorism I'm sure many of you are familiar with: "youth is wasted on the young." Well, you know what, I think the real truth is that youth is wasted on the adults.

Your Country School experience, like all good education, is about challenging boundaries, trying new ideas and new activities, expanding your horizons and understanding of the world and yourself. This, in essence, is what Mr. Huwiler's class was about. Yet, as we grow older, many of us stop challenging, stop trying new things and new ideas, stop expanding our view of the world, our sightlines. We settle into a kind of comfort zone and surround ourselves with the things and the people that serve merely to reinforce our own understanding of the way we think the world is and ought to be. In short, we stop being young people – open to the world, vulnerable, exposed – and we hunker down into the familiar, the cock-sure.

But youth, like art, is more interesting, more dynamic, more enriching. This is why I want to exhort each of you in this room today, both kid and adult, to hold on to your youthful ways of seeing a world without limits or boundaries – the far off places beyond the ridgelines just east of here that I saw as a child – of challenging and expanding your views, your skills and your talents, and in so doing, like the artist that each of you can be, creating better worlds, better realities.

According to the Hindu philosophy, nothing finishes, only changes in the continuum of eternal life. Your youth never dies, but for many of us, it is forgotten, like an old sweater you might leave behind – in this room, on the playing field, in music class.

So instead of imparting a lesson, let me close by simply encouraging you to stay always young in your spirit and outlook and to keep us adults honest and open to new ideas as we slowly harden and set, like concrete, in our adult ways. Help us nurture and keep alive the youthful energy that enables us to try new things and meet new challenges – whether world peace or environmental sustainability, poverty or racial strife – or any other formidable problem, large or small, that too many adults will claim is insoluble while labeling those who would actually undertake to solve them as "hopeless romantics" or "starry-eyed idealists" or even worse, "liberals."

Find your equivalent of the Skye Boat Song and never lose it. Keep singing it, or writing it, or painting it, but never lose it. It's what makes the Country School – its teachers, its classes, its plays and playing fields – so vital, so essential and is, in the end, nothing less than the key to creating a better world.

Thanks again for this honor and for listening this morning. I wish you all the very best of health and fortune.

Regarding the Wind

Northern Woodlands Magazine
Spring 2004

Ever since we cut down a white pine plantation on the north side of our property several years ago, the wind hasn't stopped howling. Though we lie in the shadow of a small chain of hills in the Green Mountain National Forest, all it took was the creation of a small clearing around our farmhouse to reveal just how windy the North Woods are. Countless nights I've been awakened by the sounds of our old 12-over-12 windows chattering like teeth, their decrepit glass and glazing courageously holding their own against the incessant gales.

These days, I'm not the only one regarding the wind. All across the region, from Tug Hill to Maine, the talk is of wind farms. Not surprisingly, with each proposal has followed a wave of protests by neighbors and others claiming that wind turbines on mountaintops, no matter how sleek or environmentally virtuous, are a blight on a pristine landscape, an unholy trade-off of aesthetic beauty for renewable power.

Though wind energy comprises less than one percent of the nation's power supply, the push by entrepreneurs, state and local governments, and grassroots activists to increase the production and use of renewables like wind, solar, and biomass is an important signal that many Americans are coming to realize that our dependence on nineteenth-century fuels like oil and coal, almost two-thirds of which come from outside the U.S., is not only bad for the environment but also threatens our economy and security.

Most of our power comes from large, centralized power plants that burn fossil fuels shipped in from far away to service a grid of users spread across a vast territory. By contrast, renewable power depends on the energy sources indigenous to a particular area.

Accordingly, this more decentralized, place-based system forces citizens to reckon with their energy needs in ways they've never had to, by moving the energy source itself, and not merely the energy consumption, closer to home – in Vermont, it's along Route 9, or on Mt. Equinox, or Glebe Mountain, or the Lowell Mountain range. This can be very discomforting, as the string of wind farm controversies shows.

Beyond the contested aesthetic, environmental, and economic issues associated with almost any development project, the most important question raised by wind farms is essentially a civic one: how do individuals and, by turn, communities make pattern-changing decisions, in both public policy and personal attitudes, to shift from the status quo to a better, more just, and more environmentally sound future? Debates about wind energy and other renewables are important because they compel us as locals at least to consider, if not to act on, the public interest as it plays out across several scales – from the nearby mountaintop to thousands of miles away – and to begin to think like citizens, beyond the narrow "not in my backyard" (NIMBY) stance that has become the default for most communities facing any and all new development proposals. Importantly, renewable energy is one of the few areas of our post-industrial, global capitalist culture where place – local place – still matters a lot. It depends first and foremost on local resources – natural, political, and social. Without them, there is no renewable energy future.

Now NIMBYism is in theory a good thing, a byproduct of a robustly pluralistic and open society where many voices can be heard. The trouble is, not all NIMBYism is created equal. Some is more powerful, louder than others, especially when affluent and well-connected individuals are involved. Ideally, all communities would have the same NIMBY power, the same access to the legal, political, and financial resources that make for successful NIMBY campaigns. This would mean that poor communities, the same ones who often live near older, dirty power plants, the same ones who end up sending their sons and daughters to fight wars over resources like oil, would be less vulnerable to these unwanted perils, more equal vis-à-vis their wealthier fellow citizens. In this ideal world, in turn, there would be no place left to site such polluting facilities (except in other countries, but that's another story), and communities would be forced to develop better, cleaner alternatives. But we don't live in this world, this country. We live instead in a place where the playing field is anything but level, where the people and communities who have lived at safe remove from dirty power plants and other hazards can also oppose greener alternatives, resulting in the perpetuation of distributional inequities.

New Englanders have proved to be among the most public-spirited of Americans, with wind farms but the latest test in a long line of civic challenges. As with any difficult public policy issue, there are no simple answers, only hard choices, hard work, and perseverance. My bet is that we in the Northeast will figure wind farms out – will build them in some places, not in others. And that's okay. The key is that we actually join the issue, engage as citizens in the tough decision making it demands, and come out the other end ready for the next challenge.

Vermont Housing and Conservation Board

Vermont Public Radio
November 2004

A wildlife refuge or affordable housing?
A farmfield versus a big box store?
A scenic ridge top or an assembly of wind turbines?
These simple couplets describe a few of the signal land use challenges of our time, no strangers to Vermonters, underlying which are critical trade-offs that go to the core of our definition of a just and sustainable society.
Saving wildlife, farmfields, and ridge tops is about preserving the best of our history and landscape. We resist change, trying to keep things they way they are because they're good or cherished or because change, in whatever form, can be a scary business.

Housing, big box stores and wind turbines, meanwhile, reflect our basic human need to build and not merely to preserve – be it through architecture, or commerce, or science, or public policy.

Here in Vermont, we have an institution that's simultaneously a saver and a builder. One of a handful of its kind anywhere, the Vermont Housing and Conservation Board is a state-supported funding agency with a unique mandate: to help conserve working farms and other natural and historic resources while supporting affordable housing and community development.

The Board was the brainchild not of a single person but of many – land trusts, affordable housing advocates, historic preservation groups – who came together in 1986 to form the Housing and Conservation Coalition, a smart growth organization before the term was even invented. In 1987, the law establishing the Board was enacted.

Fast forward 17 years, and today the Board has helped conserve over 325,000 acres of Vermont's countryside while underwriting the construction of roughly 7500 units of perpetually affordable housing. It has also become a national model, borrowed by states like New Jersey and Rhode Island and revered by smart growth advocates across the country.

The Board has been a key player in not just preserving Vermont's landscapes but creating places in the fullest sense, where nature and culture, past and present, wealthy and low-income are linked together by that one great denominator, the land.

As Gus Seelig, the Board's Director and one of the visionaries behind its formation, says: "Our goal has been to empower Vermont communities to conserve and develop assets – both homes and land that would maintain Vermont's historic pattern of compact village settlement surrounded by a working countryside and thriving communities for Vermonters of all backgrounds and incomes."

At a time when it seems there's little room for agreement regarding difficult public policy questions, when local communities and the nation as a whole appear divided – Blue State against Red, us versus them – the Board and its efforts are a beacon of hope. Reaching across different groups and points of view, it is a rare public voice claiming we are all united by our own common ground, by the natural resources and community assets that sustain us. Even better, it's actually proving it.

Team Work

Vermont Public Radio
February 2005

2004 was a banner year for New England sports fans, what with the Red Sox first World Series title in 86 years and the Patriot's third Superbowl ring.

Except perhaps for Pedro Martinez, the now former Sox pitcher and perennial prima donna, what set these teams apart is their team ethic. Players willing to take a back seat, make compromises, and even take pay cuts to stick together.

Sports writer after sports writer extolled this team spirit as the key to their success. Apparently, other teams have gotten the message as they look to replace over-paid superstars with lunch-pail foot soldiers.

Now consider not a sports team but a community. Isn't it curious that when it comes to accounting for a successful franchise, we're quick to celebrate team work, yet when many of us think of our own communities, we don't think in terms of a team at all, at least we don't act like we do. At a recent school board meeting in my district, budget discussions soon devolved into an us-versus-them proceeding, as if folks were from different planets, let alone points of view. Or take your average planning meeting to discuss a proposed housing project, or a big-box shopping center, or, worse yet, a wind farm; team spirit is probably the last thing that comes to mind. It's all about which side you're on, who's the enemy, and how you'll attack.

Sports are a perfect metaphor for community planning, not because they both involve competition, but for other reasons. Like sports, planning is about meeting challenges: the stakes are high, requiring stamina and skill, and there are strategies and tools that can help increase the likelihood of success, just like a Bill Belichik defensive scheme or the pitch calling of Sox catcher Jason Varitek. Planning is also by definition a team sport, it's about our ability to develop the "I" into the "We," as the sociologist Bob Putnam says. It demands that individuals check some of their self-interest at the door and open their minds to the views and needs of the larger community, their home team. This is less an intellectual exercise than it is an artful one, for it demands that people use their imaginations to step inside the shoes of their neighbor, or a developer, or even harder, someone who doesn't yet exist, the future generation.

At its best, planning is democracy's ultimate team sport, demanding at once solid individual play and highly coordinated collective action. With Vermont facing unprecedented challenges like the affordable housing crisis, skyrocketing energy bills, and rising education costs, it's high time we raised our game. And what better occasion than with spring training just getting underway.

Planning and Law

Vermont Public Radio
October 2005

It's been a few years since I called myself a lawyer. I've been a clerk to a federal judge, a law professor and I even filed a few lawsuits. But that was a while ago.

In recent years, I've found myself hanging out more with planners than lawyers. Planners are people who think about the future for a living. They're concerned with things like housing and jobs and open space and less with rules and regulations. And to a good planner, a plan is only as good as it is flexible, so it can be adjusted to changing circumstances and unforeseen consequences.

The recent confirmation of John Roberts as Chief Justice of the Supreme Court and nomination of Harriet Miers to replace Justice O'Connor got me thinking again about lawyers. With these two appointments, President Bush will have had an extraordinary opportunity to make his mark, not only on the court, but the country. After all, the Supreme Court gets to decide what the Constitution says, and thus what the culture will or will not allow, from sexual conduct to voting rights to the protection of endangered species.

President Bush has made no secret of the fact that he favors judges like Scalia and Thomas, who seek to interpret the constitution according to the framers' intent. Bush believes that, by sticking to the words of the constitution, judges can objectively divine the original intent.

But the planner in me doesn't believe a judge can simply interpret the constitution in a way that stays true to the original intent – at least not in the hard cases, which are the ones that usually wind up in court in the first place. If the meaning of the words were self-evident, there'd be no dispute, and no reason to have judges.

The bigger problem with originalism is the way it views the constitution, as something frozen in time. I prefer to view the constitution as America's greatest planning document, our master blueprint. It establishes the basic structure of our society. That it was ratified in 1787 doesn't mean that it has to be approached as if we, too, were living in the 18th century. Rather, like any good plan, the Constitution should be seen as an evolving document, one embedded in a set of immutable but general principles – like equal protection and due process – but a document that responds to the unique circumstances of the present-day. This is Justice Breyer's view; it's an honest approach, a planning approach.

I think if folks like Madison and Jefferson were around today they'd disapprove of taking a narrow view of the constitution and the role of judges, as well as judges who insist on an orthodox approach to interpretation.

I say better to have the planner's flexibility than the lawyer's formalism. I guess that's a big part of why I no longer practice law.

Bill Belichick

Perspectives on Place Blog
November 2005

"The smarter you are, the more you want to learn"

So says Ernie Accorsi, the General Manager of the New York Giants football squad. He's referring to acclaimed New England Patriots head coach Bill Belichick, known for his many forays around the National Football League talking to opposing coaches about what works, what accounts for their successes and failures. The idea is simple: knowledge exchange. As Belichick puts it, "It's just an exchange of information with somebody that you have common ground with. You talk about things that are successful, and sometimes that has an application to what you're doing."

What if community planning were like football and planners were like Belichick? What if delegations of civic leaders went from peer community to peer community in search of excellence, of the policies and practices that account for successful outcomes according to a set of desired goals, like affordable housing, public transportation, greenspace and parks, quality schools and vibrant downtowns?

It seems to me the planning field (like the football field) is in need of this kind of sharing, peer-to-peer. It should be standard practice for local officials and citizens' groups to travel from place to place to meet with others whose planning experiences offer fresh insight and information that can be brought back home.

Our recent Community Planning Collaborative event in Orlando, Florida is an example of this. About 150 planners, designers, policymakers and citizens from around the country joined with over 50 local officials and residents to help the City of Orlando and Orange County figure out a set of challenging planning issues related to new development in this fast growing part of the state. For three days, we poured over maps, kibitzed over dinner and generally learned from eachother about different approaches to land use and development. Instead of traveling from community to community (the Belichick model), we gathered in one place, bringing a host of different perspectives to bear on Orlando's and the county's situation.

The larger point here is that to do things differently, we need to perceive them differently, and to do this, we need to take ourselves out of our normal context, our comfort zone, and shake things up. This, in essence, is what exploration is all about: finding new worlds by stepping outside of old ones.

We don't need to reinvent or start from scratch; we need to borrow and imitate. There's nothing new under the sun. As John Thackara describes in his provocative and timely book, In the Bubble: Designing for a Complex World, innovation is the process of reusing and recombining smartly, creatively. We innovate, he says, when we learn to learn from the world (Ian McHarg's idea of designing for nature, or the industrial ecology model which seeks to mimic the forms and functions of natural systems in industrial ones) and our own neighbors, be they across the street or across the globe. Innovation as alchemy.

Maybe it's just me, but sometimes it seems we're far more innovative when it comes to things like football, ice cream (Chunky Monkey, Phish Food and Cherry Garcia come to mind), and I-pods than we are about our own communities. This is a variation on Leopold's notion that "to build a better motor, we tap the uttermost powers of the human brain; to build a better countryside, we throw dice."

I think we need to take many pages from Belichick's playbook and start learning from eachother. From community visits to learning networks to creative convenings, we have the learning tools. We need to start using them more.

David Bollier

Perspectives on Place Blog
December 2005

I had a great chat last week with David Bollier, co-founder of the group Public Knowledge and editor of Onthecommons.org. David's helping lead the charge to reclaim the idea, if not the reality, of the commons in American life, the shared places and spaces – physical, social and intellectual – that really matter to vital communities and democracy itself. They are the middle ground between those two behemoths we call the market and the state. David's one of the stalwart voices sticking up for the "We" when it seems so many of the most outspoken are all about the "I" – privatizing parks, gating-up subdivisions, locking up ideas in the vault of intellectual property law.

"Citizens," David explains, "often fail to see the hidden wealth of 'hometown commons' – an independent business sector, community supported agriculture, good parks and libraries, community festivals, farmers' markets, local currencies and robust voluntary sectors. Supporting the 'social wealth' of hometown commons is an urgent priority for our times." This is what makes David's message so strong: it's folksy, not abstract or rarified.

Right on, David. We join you in the crusade for the commons.

December

Vermont Public Radio
December 2005

December's a very existential time for me. My birthday's in December, so as I've gotten older, I've come to approach the month with a bit of trepidation. And something about the short days and long nights adds to the unease. Being at the end of the year doesn't help either. Finality. For some reason, I always hear Wallace Stevens in my head, those last lines of "Sunday Morning":

> And, in the isolation of the sky
> At evening, casual flocks of pigeons make
> Ambiguous undulations as they sink
> Downward to darkness, on extended wings.

It's my birthday. I should be soaring, but somehow, having just past 40 in the season of the solstice, it feels more like a free fall.

But it's not just my birthday that makes me think on the meaning of life this time of year. It's also the onset of what we now politely call "the holidays." I grew up Jewish in a largely gentile community. My parents, neither of whom was very devout, couldn't quite figure out what do with Christmas and so they did what most red-blooded Americans did in the 1960s: they bought a Christmas tree. They did it for their kids. They didn't want us to feel left out.

Meanwhile, we also lit Hanukah candles for eight nights, the two traditions living awkwardly side by side, neither one of them fully embraced, or understood.

Fast forward a few decades and I find myself in a similar situation, but with a twist. I married a non-Jew who, like me, can only be regarded as a secularist but who, come the season, insists on having a tree. She claims it's for the benefit of our two young children, but I think she does it for herself. I'm now part of the ritual, striking out each early December, saw in hand, to the nearby tree farm to cut the perfect Balsam. So much for my tree hugger status.

There's no way around it: this time of year forces me to ask some big questions: Who am I, Jew or gentile? And is it really the parent in me that participates in the rite of this season or, like my wife, the child within the parent who's reminded unfailingly that December is the month of the longest darkness, that with each tree I cut down I'm losing something, another year?

I think I'm beginning to realize that my annual bout with existentialism is actually a birthday present disguised as anxiety. It's the time when I receive the gift of reaffirming my own humanity – the connection to my past, to others who are different from me and to the light that always shines brightest in the darkness.

Fact Free Zones

Vermont Public Radio
January 2006

I was recently given a copy of James Frey's best-selling memoir, *A Million Little Pieces*. No sooner had I started it than reports began to surface about Frey's alleged fabrication of many key facts in his story. Since those early charges, Frey's all but confessed to playing fast and loose with the truth in his supposedly non-fiction account of violence, addiction and recovery.

Nevertheless, Frey and his publisher are defending the memoir, as is Oprah Winfrey, who selected it for her book club last fall. Acknowledging the fakery, Winfrey has stated publicly she still regards it as a must-read.

The facts, it seems, aren't as important as an entertaining narrative, something moving or dramatic.

But the publishing world isn't the only place where facts are vulnerable. Attend any planning meeting on a controversial issue and chances are good you'll find yourself entering what I call a "Fact Free Zone." Fact Free Zones are places where certain irrefutable principles or realities – the laws of physics, perhaps, or economic facts such as skyrocketing housing costs – fall prey to the whims and passions of people determined to deny them. Fact Free Zones are what happens when planning officials decline to enforce high standards of behavior in public meetings and when individuals, upon setting foot in those meetings, fail to own up to their civic responsibility to engage their fellow citizens respectfully and with a curious mind in discussions about important public policy choices.

Much like Frey's memoir, Fact Free Zones depend on compelling narratives, but rather than having one author, these stories have many. They're the stories people tell themselves that are immune to empirical data and alternative views. They're mental models clad in steel, helmet-sized echo chambers that reinforce people's comforting myths and misperceptions.

Like the idea that low-income housing will make communities less safe, or that gated neighborhoods will make them safer. Or that an aging population is not siphoning New England of the brains and bodies needed to sustain it, with almost a quarter of the region's 20 to 34 year olds having fled in the 1990s. Or how about the notion that a warming climate is somebody else's business, not something local communities and each of us as individuals need to worry about.

Now I'm no objectivist; I believe that facts are invariably colored by one's values and experience, and that claims to truth need to be evaluated with a skeptical eye. I'm more of a pragmatist in the mold of the Vermonter John Dewey. Truth, Dewey held, is contingent, not transcendent. But just because a fact might not be universally true doesn't mean it can be dismissed.

We who live here are the principal authors of New England's future. We can elect to write fiction, spinning amusing tales like James Frey that make us feel good but at the same time deceive us. Or we can be honest and deal in facts. It's a harder story to write, but it's one we and our children will be proud to read.

Promise of Paradox

Vermont Public Radio
February 2006

I recently gave a talk about social change to a group of graduate students. Here they were, the country's best and brightest, from all walks of life and armed with knowledge and experience unrivaled by their forebears. And yet, as is often the case, I found myself barraged after my remarks with a flurry of despairing, almost cynical, questions. "OK, positive change has happened in our society," a young woman, born in New Delhi and raised in California, conceded, "but that was before 9/11, before the Iraq War and the distracting threat of terror. Just look at the recent rollback of so many important social programs," she bemoaned, "or the growing gap between rich and poor, or the menace of global climate change. Do you really think we can solve these problems?" Like many of her peers, she seemed defeated before she'd even begun.

As I was leaving the auditorium I found myself reciting Dickens: "It was the best of times, it was the worst of times." Never before has there been a generation so well equipped to navigate the choppy waters of modern life. They're smarter, more worldly, more technologically capable and better informed than most adults I know. They have at their disposal all manner of tools, from technology like the internet and computers to degrees from the world's finest universities, each of which brings access to knowledge and power from which anything is possible. And still, many of them feel disempowered and hopeless.

The contrast between the reality of the students' immense capabilities and their perceived powerlessness is one of the great paradoxes of our times. How can it be that the best and worst, the brightest and darkest, sit side by each so comfortably?

Paradox, I believe, is the cardinal truth of our age. Just look around; it's everywhere. We live amidst unspeakable terrors and yet have never been safer; the globalizing forces of commerce and communications have given rise to a grassroots surge toward localism and self-reliance; rural communities are embracing dense settlements and vibrant downtowns while cities are restoring long-neglected greenspaces and celebrating farmers' markets. The list goes on at dizzying length.

Paradox is really just another name for the tension that resides in all of us, the contradictory impulses and beliefs that can alternately deflate or invigorate us. It is, at bottom, a creative tension that, like a motor, propels us from one state of being to the next, making the very act of change possible, if not inexorable. Paradox is the corner about to be turned.

The magnitude and complexity of today's challenges are real and formidable. But so is our ability to meet them head on, and that ability is only increasing. The question is, will we allow ourselves to be defeated by our paradoxes or energized by them?

Next time I speak to a group of students about social change, I'll be sure to ask them this question before they ask me theirs. Just call it a preemptive strike.

Muir and Pinchot

Vermont Public Radio
March 2006

Listening to all the brickbats thrown at the new plan to add 27,000 acres to the Green Mountain National Forest, has in turn thrown me into a time warp. The year is 1913, and the warring parties are John Muir and Gifford Pinchot, their gloves off, sparring over the fate of the Hetch Hetchy Valley in California's Yosemite National Park.

Muir, the Scottish-born mountaineer and founder of the Sierra Club, was the prototypical romantic environmentalist. For him, wilderness was a tonic, a refuge from the depredations of industrial society. He denounced those he saw as exploiting nature for material gain, like the politicians and businessmen who wanted to build a reservoir for San Francisco in the Hetch Hetchy Valley. Decrying the proposal, Muir declared "everybody needs beauty as well as bread, places to play in and pray in where nature may heal and cheer and give strength to body and soul alike."

Pinchot was Muir's perfect foil. A forester by training, he was the first head of the U.S. Forest Service and promoted the sustainable use of natural resources, what came to be known as progressive conservation. Ever the scientist, he ridiculed Muir's romanticism as mere sentimentalism. "The object of our forest policy," he wrote, "is not to preserve the forests because they are beautiful . . . but the making of prosperous homes. . . . The first great fact about conservation is that it stands for development." Pinchot adamantly supported the Hetch Hetchy project, which was built, after years of wrangling, in 1913.

And so it goes. Criticizing the Green Mountain forest plan for allowing too much logging and off-road vehicle use, one environmentalist reprised Muir's mantra. "Wilderness," he said, "offers an opportunity to experience solitude and quiet recreation away from [our] busy lives." Meanwhile, unhappy loggers, ATV riders and hunters claim that the plan effectively shuts them out of the forest, leaving them too little timber, road access and open habitat for their tax dollars.

Romanticism versus resource extraction. Tree-loving versus tree-cutting. Muir versus Pinchot. A century later, the terms of the debate sound much the same.

But the debate itself begs a more fundamental question: Is there another way of looking at the forest, as something other than a pristine refuge on the one hand or millions of marketable board feet on the other?

Perhaps we should heed the advice of a group in Corinth who publish Northern Woodlands magazine. They encourage environmentalists and forest workers to speak to each other respectfully and with a shared appreciation for the forest's many uses. They provide a forum where reverence for the woods meets the reality of making a living from them, where tree-huggers like me can find their inner chain-saw and where loggers can learn about woodlands ecology and sustainable forestry. It really is a new way of looking at the forest. No brickbats allowed.

I like to think that if Muir and Pinchot were around today they'd both embrace this idea of a shared vision. But I wonder: Will Vermonters do the same?

Jane Jacobs

Perspectives on Place Blog
April 2006

April is truly the cruelest month. Or at least, with the news of Jane Jacobs' death, the saddest. I had the great pleasure of getting to know Jane back in 2000 via a conference in her honor I helped organize with my Boston College Law School colleague Zyg Plater and a group of law students (BC houses her papers). We stayed in touch, though infrequently.

This from *The Death and Life of Great American Cities*, her magnum opus:

> It may be romantic to search for the salves of society's ills in slow-moving rustic surroundings, or among innocent, unspoiled provincials, if such exist, but it is a waste of time. Does anyone suppose that, in real life, answers to any of the great questions that worry us today are going to come out of homogeneous settlements?
>
> Dull, inert cities, it is true, do contain seeds of their own destruction and little else. But lively, diverse, intense cities contain the seeds of their own regeneration, with energy enough to carry over for problems and needs outside themselves.

Impassioned and opinionated, Jane was a maverick, a genius, a curmudgeon, a celebrator, an urbanist, an ecologist, a peace activist, an intellectual, a citizen planner and so many other things. She got us thinking about sidewalks and busy streets, to be sure, but she really got us thinking about our collective soul, the spirit that animates and energizes our places, that gives them life and authenticity.

The death and life. . . . The title seems so fitting now. d souls of every community worthy of the name. Long live Jane Jacobs.

Mountain School

Vermont Public Radio
October 2006

It was an odd scene at the Peru Town Hall on a recent evening, where about 60 people gathered to hear about a proposed new campus for Burr & Burton Academy, our local high school just down the hill in Manchester. Burr & Burton, it turns out, is bucking Vermont's trend of declining school enrollments, and thanks to projected increases, is hoping to expand its facilities by creating a 100-acre wilderness school where, for one semester, 70 students would be immersed in learning about Vermont's wild side. Housed in a state-of-the-art green building and surrounded by national forest, the students would have an educational experience unlike any other in the state.

What was strange, however, was who showed up at the meeting. There was only one kid. Most were senior citizens who long ago said farewell to school lunches and PTA meetings. For many of them, the idea of a new school in their midst is an unwelcome trip down memory lane. Been there, done that.

Others were part-timers with second homes. They're more than happy to think of Peru as a "child-free zone." They already live in communities with kids, schools and big yellow buses and have a hard time reconciling their idea of a quiet, mountain setting with a vibrant campus bustling with tree-hugging teens.

Parents with school-age kids, like me, were in the clear minority. I counted only five, but we were all excited by the proposal. At a time when towns across the state are agonizing over school closings, the idea that Peru might play host to a new one, to say nothing of its visionary program, seems almost revolutionary.

But it's actually more than that. A school is a community's premier symbol of its own survival, of its ability to reproduce itself over time as a living, breathing, thinking place. This is why a community that loses it's school often feels it's also lost its identity. It's like losing a vital organ or worse, its soul.

To see a school disappear is, for a moment, to see a community's life flash before its eyes.

But a new school is just the opposite. It's a life-giving force, an affirmation of the future. Tracy Black, the town clerk, summed it up best. Reciting the latest figures from Peru's Grand List, she noted that, of the 600 plus properties on the list, only about one-fifth of them are full-timers. The community, she sighed, is slowly withering away; the school is, to her, an occasion for hope.

The last time Peru had a school the Vietnam War was still raging. A photograph of its final graduating class hangs in a glass case in the Town Hall. When I think about Peru's future, I wonder if the town itself will one day become a memory, an image on display, or will the town persevere? And then I imagine the sound of school buses. To me, they sound like a heart beating.

Part-Time Vermonters

Vermont Public Radio
December 2006

It was early Sunday morning a few weeks ago when I passed a local motel and saw, out of the corner of my eye, three people duck into a large green van with the markings of a local resort on the door. Sunlight reflected off the wet blacktop, but the air was cold. In spite of this, the three were so lightly dressed that they had wrapped themselves up in blankets to ward off the chill. They looked confused, like refugees at some remote border crossing.

But they were not refugees; they were part-time Vermonters, as essential to Vermont's economy as their other seasonal counterparts – tourists and second-home owners – whose hotel rooms they clean, groceries they bag and tables they wait. They're West Indians, South Americans, Africans, Vietnamese and Bosnians. They work hard, provide for their families and practice religion. Many come from traditional agricultural societies going back centuries.

And yet, as seasonal workers who often lack the most basic financial and educational resources, they're an orphaned class, even here in egalitarian Vermont. Unlike the thousands of illegal immigrants who work on the state's dairy farms, resort and service industry staff qualify for the guest worker program that allows foreigner nationals to hold seasonal jobs. Even so, many can only manage to eak out a marginal living. They sleep on floors in poorly heated rooms. And without their own transport in a heavily auto-dependent state, they have to be shuttled from place to place.

Today, immigrants in the U.S. make up about 12 percent of the total population, more than double what it was just 50 years ago. And they're more visible than ever, having leapfrogged the traditional gateway cities like New York and Los Angeles for new destinations: the rural south, the Midwest. Vermont.

Not surprisingly, immigration has become a hot button issue.

Suddenly immigrants are everywhere. But then again, they always have been. After all, we're a nation of newcomers, save for the Native Americans whose plight reminds us that the claim to being here first guarantees nothing.

And isn't that the problem? Though most of us have been here just a few generations, we act as if we own the joint. Yet, immigrants have always fueled the culture, made it vital. A century ago it was in big cities like New York, Chicago and San Francisco. Today, it's in the metro areas of states like North Carolina, Nevada, Colorado and New Hampshire. As go the immigrants, so goes the action.

I think of those three people clutching blankets to stay warm on their early morning commute and I wish we could do better. As a state known for its homogeneity and aging population, I would think that Vermonters would eagerly embrace new immigrants and the new energy they bring with them.

In my vision for Vermont's future, honest work will be rewarded with pay sufficient to meet basic needs. Willing workers, of every color and creed, will be welcome and second-class citizenship will be yesterday's problem.

Social Innovation

Vermont Public Radio
March 2007

I'm no economist, but I can't help following closely what's going on in the US economy right now. Two stories in particular have caught my eye.

The first is the decline and imminent fall of Detroit and the Big 3 automakers. Thirty years ago Detroit's CEOs and unions demanded the Japanese build factories in the US or face further import restrictions. Today, the Japanese have not only complied, but thrived. They've built a superior product and continue to innovate with technologies like hybrid engines. Most important, they've responded to what consumers want: fuel efficiency, good design and low maintenance costs. Some, like Honda, have even taken maverick stances on issues like emissions caps, building a constituency among progressive consumers while the Big 3 fight tooth and nail against such reforms.

Now turn the page in the Business Section of your newspaper and you'll read about the travails of another keystone American institution, Hollywood. It turns out the big movie studios can no longer depend on domestic sales for their profits. Instead, they're relying increasingly on foreign box office revenues. For a variety of reasons, quality chief among them, Americans are declining to buy what Hollywood has to offer.

So what's the connection between Detroit and Hollywood, two cities and two industries that could hardly be more different?

It's that what these sacred cows of American culture produce is being rejected by the American people. Sure, there's still a ton of leading edge, world-class businesses in the

US, but the foreign competition is heating up, especially in traditional strongholds.

But perhaps Detroit and Hollywood's loss is society's gain. We may have ceded our creative edge in industries like automobile manufacturing and filmmaking but we have a chance to make up for it in what I think is the next frontier of American ingenuity – social innovation.

Social innovations are new ways of governing our society that maximize opportunities for people to realize their personal and collective potential. They're the strategies and institutions that operate among the public, private and non-profit sectors to enable our increasingly diverse, post-industrial society to pursue a vision of a just and sustainable world – one person, one community at a time. They are employee-owned companies, tax credits for renewable energy technologies, zoning rules that promote dense, vibrant downtowns and free wireless internet access. Social innovations serve one master: solving social problems.

Many of the tools of social innovation already exist. The challenge is to develop the civic will to use them at scale, to build a new social order out of them.

General Motors claims in a current ad, that a new American revolution is upon us. I agree. But it's not a car or a truck. Rather, as in 1776, it's the way we govern ourselves, the rules and institutions we put in place to achieve a better society. And like the original, today's revolution needs leaders up to the challenge, less like Lee Iacocca or Michael Eisner and more in the mold of George Washington and Thomas Jefferson.

Treehugger

Vermont Public Radio
May 2007

Last month's devastating storm that left many of Rutland's trees in shambles brought me back to the urban forest I used to call home. I cut my teeth as a treehugger on the mean streets of New York's Lower East Side. Whereas some of my tree-crazy colleagues chose to lash themselves to ancient Coastal Redwoods in the remote wilds of northern California, I opted for the chain-linked tangle of the Bowery's Liz Christie garden where, as a member of the Green Guerrillas, one of the nation's oldest urban green groups, I organized street tree tours for New Yorker's eager to learn the difference between a linden and a lamp post. And I've been doing them ever since, in every city I've lived in.

On each tour, I start with the same simple question: "What's the average life span of a street tree?"

Invariably, the answers are wildly optimistic and, regrettably, wrong. No, it's not 30 years, or 20, or even ten. The answer, give or take, is seven years. Which explains why I'm both delighted and concerned about the unprecedented push for tree planting in some of our biggest cities like New York, whose plans to grow their urban forest by one million trees over the coming years were recently announced to great fanfare.

One study found that New York's trees provide an annual financial benefit of around $122 million, with every dollar spent on trees generating more than five times that amount in benefits, like providing shade, cleaning polluted run-off and absorbing carbon dioxide, a plus for combating climate change.

But the challenge of city trees has never been about their

value; it's about maintaining that value over time, about literally keeping the trees alive. As with any infrastructure investment, the hard part comes after the initial construction is completed – who's going to maintain the trees and how much will that maintenance cost?

The problem with street trees, unlike the trees of Vermont's mountain forests, is that the more you plant, the greater the maintenance required, which is no easy assignment. By their nature, urban trees are almost constantly under threat, from dogs, cars, poor soils and, of course, the weather. Further, caring for city trees demands both expertise and patience; each tree and each tree pit is like a single potted plant, needing plenty of attention.

Maintenance is a dirty word when it comes to public investment, but in the case of the urban forest, it's the only thing that matters. Better to have a city of a thousand healthy, mature trees – whose spreading crowns and root systems provide the bulk of the urban forest's benefits – than a city of a million dying saplings.

While we can't do much about the wind and weather, we can hold our cities and ourselves accountable for our trees, not just by planting them, but making sure they stick around a good, long time.

Entergy Is Not the Enemy in the Energy Debate

The Burlington Free Press
May 2007

My son's lacrosse coach, Brett, grew up in the southeast Vermont town of Vernon, home to Vermont Yankee, the nuclear power plant responsible for over one-third of Vermont's electricity. Watching our six-year olds at a recent scrimmage, Brett and I found ourselves talking about the legislature's proposal to triple the tax on Entergy, the plant's owner, over the next several years to underwrite new energy efficiency and renewable energy programs. The $25 million tax is the centerpiece of the proposed climate change bill designed to put Vermont on the path to a sustainable energy future. A school administrator who only recently moved back to his home state after a long absence, Brett couldn't understand why Vermont, which has put nuclear power at the forefront of its energy strategy for decades, would now single out Entergy to solve a problem, as he put it, of Vermonters' own making.

I've been working in the environmental trenches for two decades as a lawyer, non-profit leader and educator. In all these years, I have witnessed few environmental policy debates as misguided as this one. Like Brett, I'm left wondering about Vermonters' willingness to own up to our decisions and, more importantly, to learn from them.

For the past 35 years, Vermont Yankee has been the major provider of Vermont's electricity service, it's 650-megawatt generating capacity the mainstay of the state's energy supply. Despite perennial opposition from anti-nuclear groups and the fierce backlash against nuclear energy following the Three

Mile Island melt-down in 1979, Vermonters have continued to support the plant's dominant position in the state's energy marketplace.

Meanwhile, during the same 35-year span, we've done little to diversify our energy portfolio. Instead, Vermont contracted with another large energy provider, Canada's massive Hydro-Quebec plant, to supply another third of our electricity needs. Do the math and you discover two-thirds of the state's electricity comes from two sources.

Vermont's current energy predicament is not the result of Entergy's failure to pay its fair share of property taxes, as many of the climate change bill's supporters suggest, nor is the fact that Vermonter's generate more nuclear waste per capita, as a recent study finds, a valid reason for requiring Entergy alone to fund the expansion of the state's Efficiency Vermont program. The problem, in other words, is not Entergy; the problem is us.

To forge a sustainable energy future, Vermonters must first recognize that our demand for electricity and our choices about how we will meet that demand are at the root of the issue, and the starting point for change. We need to be creative, move beyond the monolithic energy system we ourselves constructed and stop blaming the energy industry for giving us exactly what we've asked for.

Just look at Cambridge, Massachusetts. In March, the city launched a $70 million energy efficiency fund, an Efficiency Vermont for Cambridge, to conserve energy in every building in the city. But rather than imposing a new tax on energy suppliers to pay for the program, the Cambridge Energy Alliance is raising funds from a variety of private sources – from financial institutions to foundations – with the help of an investment bank. Why can't Vermonters do the same?

Then there are folks like Middlebury's Anders Holm, who wants to build a hydroelectric plant on the Otter

Creek. He's part of a growing corps of entrepreneurs and community leaders ready to harness their towns' indigenous energy resources with micro-dams, small wind turbines, biomass plants and other technologies that collectively could make a real dent in Vermont's nuclear and big-hydro diet. Undeveloped in-state hydro alone amounts to 174,000 kilowatts, or roughly 22 percent more than Vermont currently uses. Local energy systems are a strong antidote to an undiversified, and unsustainable, state energy supply.

Next time I see my friend Brett, I think I'll tell him about Anders Holm. Who knows, maybe he'll want to return to Vernon and start his own energy project. Better yet, maybe Entergy will help him.

Border Crossing

Vermont Public Radio
June 2007

Emma Lazarus would not be pleased.

As I waited to cross the border at Derby Line on the way back from a recent trip with my family to Quebec City, I couldnt help but notice the peeling paint and rust covering every square inch of the U.S. Customs facility, an outdated steel erector-set of a structure. My brief moment of patriotic pride the one that happens, as if preternaturally, whenever I reenter the U.S. from abroad – was quickly eroded by the ungainly reality of the dilapidated building. This was no golden door welcoming the huddled masses, Lazarus's immortal words describing our most famous port of entry, the Statue of Liberty; it was an embarrassment.

How could it be, I thought, that a nation forged by immigrants into the wealthiest civilization in the history of humankind could let even one of its gateways and symbols of America's hope and promise, corrode into a just a pile of rusting slag, an insult to the very notion of immigration, to say nothing of public space and border protection?

As I handed the customs agent my passport, I pointed to the blight and, trying not to offend, expressed my disappointment as a taxpayer and citizen. As if relieved to hear my complaint, the man agreed wholeheartedly, as did his fellow agent, who happened to walk by. They both expressed the wish for a remedy for what to them is what for them is not only an important federal facility but an unhealthy, uninspiring work environment.

The author Salmon Rushdie has said that immigration is the great story of the last century. As the first decade of the twenty-first century comes to a close, immigration remains a signal story, a hot button for everyone from nativist politicians eager to scapegoat illegal immigrants for society's ills to Vermont farmers and ski resort owners who depend on seasonal labor for their businesses.

But if immigration is a deeply contested political and economic matter, its place at the heart of our American narrative is indisputable. Its the cherished idea of immigration, of people moving at great risk from one place to another in search of a better life, that makes this building more than just another toll booth and that gives the traveler pause as he crosses the invisible line between who he is and who he might have been.

Driving away from the border, I was struck by the irony of how much we're spending on controversial new fences on the Mexican border - never mind $430 billion for the war in Iraq, all in the name of homeland security. Meanwhile, back home many of the very buildings already securing our borders are deteriorating. Makes me wonder what other facilities and programs, full of important social meaning and purpose, are falling apart?

Part II : Place

I'm a place guy. Place is what happens when people inhabit space and make it their own. It's the sum of their feelings, beliefs, practices and policies, embedded and expressed in the built, the natural and everything in between. Place is where the feedback loops are tightest, where what happens anywhere in the world comes home to roost – on your front doorstep, on Main Street, on the local ridgeline. The proverbial backyard.

So begins a chapter I wrote called "Coming Home to Roost" in *Ignition: What You Can Do to Fight Global Warming and Spark a Movement.* From the small to the big, place is the vector by which individuals connect up and create solidarity with their world – next door or 10,000 miles away. As Gary Snyder reminds us, in the form of landscape, place is the "one deep thing [we] share" amidst all that divides us – race, ideology, class, religion. It is the act of being present, of investing feeling as well as reason, in a physical and social space outside our own skin. It is the gesture of forming attachments to something we often cannot even describe but can only experience or feel.

Places are shaped and distinguished by an array of forces – some mysterious, others as conspicuous as a sore thumb. And those forces are constantly in play, internal to external, social to environmental, technological to meteorological. Place and places in the U.S. are a complex mixture, at once distinct and bounded yet part of an economic system that pays scant attention to fixed borders or the particulars of local culture, geography or history. Today, that system looms larger than ever, challenging the very idea of place as a viable framework with which to understand and interpret present-day American, and global, society.

Brownfields to greenfields, urban to rural, Red State to Blue State, indigenous to invasive, wilderness to Wall Street – the lexicon of place is expansive. But does it define a rigid order of discrete, differentiated zones or a more fluid, dynamic whole, each part influencing and being influenced by the other? Do the continuous streams of people, goods, information and capital in today's New Economy necessarily erode the unique contours of place, reducing them to some lowest common denominator, or do they actually help enhance them, make places more livable and interesting?

Building on the themes and perspectives explored in Part I, Part II looks at the idea, experience and practice of place and placemaking. The writings in this chapter examine the features and attitudes that constitute a place, make one place different from another and sustain or diminish it over time. It addresses the different kinds of threats and changes – real and perceived – that can undermine a community's sense of place and cause it to respond, creatively and opportunistically or, as is so often the case, in a knee-jerk way, from the gut more than the head and heart. Finally, Part II attempts to describe and define the new kinds of places – where ecology, economy and culture are viewed as the essential, interconnected building blocks for vibrant communities – signaling at last the arrival of sustainability as the keystone for a new twenty-first century American redevelopment plan.

A Green Approach to the Incinerator Site

The Boston Globe
July 1998

This summer's record-breaking rains have given the Boston area a supersize case of water on the knee. Because of the city's vast amounts of impervious surfaces like roads and parking lots that prevent effective drainage, when the heavens open up, water quickly becomes the landscape's dominant feature.

Ironically, we find ourselves in a city with place names that recall a time when the area was still blessed with wetlands and bays, the very natural systems that serve to drain and shed torrential rains. The Fenway, the Back Bay, South Bay, the Muddy River, and Fort Point Channel are a sample of the once-thriving wetlands and waterways that today are barely noticeable, if at all, beneath the city's sprawl.

Beginning in the mid-1800s, those ecosystems disappeared, giving way to development brought about by industrialization and population growth. The same forces made Boston a great cosmopolitan center in the 19th century, the hub of the universe. No longer so prominent, Boston today is trying to make a comeback and reclaim its place among the pantheon of "world class" cities.

Interestingly, this drama is being played out on the South Boston waterfront, where Bostonians are reckoning as never before with the potential trade-off between economic growth and status on the one hand and environmental quality on the other. Viewed as the last environmental frontier, the waterfront has inspired great passion regarding Boston's fate.

But the waterfront isn't the only place where Boston's destiny is at issue. Just a stone's throw away in South Bay, the filled tideland over which the Massachusetts Bay Colony's first governor's mansion is still perched in lower Roxbury, an opportunity is emerging to restore both environmental quality and economic vitality to a hard-hit district.

The South Bay Incinerator, shut down in 1975, is finally coming down after two decades of neglect. A symbol of the physical and economic decline of the area, its demolition this summer signals a new era. Though the waters of the South Bay will likely never return (unless global warming has its way), the incinerator site and nearby abandoned parcels could be redeveloped as an eco-industrial park.

These state-of-the-art facilities incorporate production methods and designs that mimic the reuse, recycling, and replenishing functions of natural systems, like wetlands, thus reducing or minimizing altogether waste and pollution.

By converting one firm's waste into another's energy, avoiding the use of toxic chemicals, using recyled rather than virgin materials, and employing energy-efficient designs, "eco-development" simultaneously protects the environment while ensuring economic growth and job opportunities.

In Manchester, N.H., the Stonyfield Farm Yogurt Co. is planning the region's first eco-industrial park, and in the South Bronx, a community development corporation and an environmental group are developing a state-of-the-art paper recycling plant on an abandoned rail yard.

Eco-development projects like these are popping up in cities and towns across the country as communities try to repair their degraded environment while bolstering their local economy.

As a brownfield or contaminated site, the South Bay Incinerator site is a perfect setting for an eco-development project, and a diverse coalition of community, business, and environmental organizations called Neighborhoods United for the South Bay is working with legislators to promote such innovative redevelopment. In light of the current strong economic conditions, the organization wants to strike while the iron is hot, hoping to transform the blighted site into a model eco-industrial use that will serve as a beacon for future redevelopment.

As the rains and flooding continue, as inevitably they will, we should see in Boston's watery past its vibrant future. Though we cannot reclaim much of the wetlands and bays that were sacrificed to development long ago, we can look to eco-development as a way of improving environmental quality while achieving economic growth.

Like the South Boston waterfront, South Bay can become a symbol of not only Boston's commercial might but also its environmental health.

The Old Growth Among Us

Northern Woodlands Magazine
Fall 2001

Near an old farmhouse in Vermont I recently discovered
several acres of the most magnificent trees I've ever seen.
Towering close to 100 feet above the formidable understory
of white birch and balsam fir, many of their limbs sheered
off by storm and chance, a cluster of ancient sugar maples
close to three centuries old bears witness to history on this
former high sheep meadow. Thankfully, such discoveries
are becoming more frequent across the region. From the
Adirondacks and Connecticut River Valley to the White
Mountains, old growth hardwood and conifer stands are
being reported with increasing frequency in the region,
ratcheting up the estimated amount of these arboreal treasure
troves to well over a half-million acres.

But centuries-old trees are not confined to parks or
woodlands alone. Though perhaps less visually dramatic than
their country cousins, "urban old growth" is an invaluable
part of New England's natural and cultural heritage. These
are trees on city sidewalks and in backyards that have beaten
the odds, approaching or occasionally surpassing 100 years in
age despite the fact that the average life span of most big city
street trees is barely 10 years.

Take a walk down Cambridge Street near Inman Square in
the densely packed city of Cambridge, Massachusetts. There,
just on the right as you approach the square from the west,
soars a tulip tree (liriodendron tulipifera) some 75 feet to the
firmament, providing shade and moisture to an otherwise
desertified streetscape and, come late spring, offering up
hundreds of delicate but brilliant orange and yellow blossoms
that carpet the street and sidewalk in color (the tree is a

member of the Magnolia family, after all). For nearly a century, this tree has stood as a gateway to Inman Square, a welcoming sight to residents and visitors alike. Some pray to it, others simply stand in awe, but no one who passes by can ignore its presence.

The tulip tree is one of just a handful of "witness" trees extant in Cambridge (not counting the well-cultivated trees of Harvard University, Mt. Auburn cemetery and other park-like campuses). Like their more rustic counterparts, the historic, aesthetic, and environmental benefits such urban old growth provides are beyond valuation. In terms of dollars, several studies have found that these trees add up to 25 percent to nearby property values. With so many street trees falling prey to disease (observe the great, vase-shaped American elms succumbing, one by one, to Dutch Elm disease), neglect or outright violence, such trees cry out for protection as among the few remaining natural monuments to an earlier time, a less car-infested, less paved-over age. What these trees lack in extent or number, they make up for with their miraculous durability.

Perhaps it is this that inspires such great passion in urban residents for their old arbor. Unfortunately, development pressures and property rights leave these trees highly vulnerable. Just a few weeks ago, a woman chained herself to the Cambridge tulip tree to stop a neighbor from cutting it down, a few inches of the tree's root flare having extended onto her driveway. Whether it's an ancient redwood California or a tulip tree in Cambridge, it seems nothing short of passion can save them.

But more can be done. In Massachusetts, urban old growth is protected by the public shade tree statute, a century-old law that, though little known, requires city tree wardens to take extra measures to save trees that provide shade and other benefits on or near public rights of way. In addition, local historic commissions have the power to designate special trees as landmarks owing to their unique environmental, cultural or aesthetic benefits. Though rarely used for this purpose, landmarking authority is potentially a great shield in the fight to preserve urban old growth, converting what are almost always informal landmarks into official ones. To the extent that developers and property owners fail to realize the economic value of old trees, these tools give communities the power to protect the trees' other values.

As the red-hot economy continues to encroach on every last inch of developable land in Massachusetts and other New England cities, residents and public officials would do well to consider the countless benefits of the old growth among us, and make use of tools like the shade tree law and landmarking process to protect them, not only for the stories they tell about our past, but for what they say about who we are today.

The Case for Good Zoning

Conservation Matters Magazine
Spring 2002

I lead a double life. During the week, my family and I live in Cambridge, Massachusetts, one of New England's most densely settled and culturally diverse cities – in the heart of the region's largest metropolitan area. Come most weekends, we retreat to an old farmhouse in the southern Vermont hamlet of Belmont. It's in the Green Mountain National Forest, just outside a small village where working dairy farms, a general store, and a few wayward moose can still be found. While the two communities could not be more different, they share a disturbing feature: they're both losing the essential qualities that make them distinctive places, owing to the same insidious force – the highest bidder.

In Cambridge, the red-hot real estate market of the last several years has driven housing prices to record levels, making the city unaffordable to all but the wealthiest homebuyers. Our modest condominium, in a three unit mid-Cambridge Victorian is worth nearly twice what we paid for it five years ago. It would be out of our price range were we in the home-buying market today. The dearth of affordable housing in a city without available land for new housing development is turning Cambridge into an exclusive enclave where only corporate executives, celebrity academics, and those lucky enough to buy in before the boom can afford to live. What used to be called "The People's Republic of Cambridge" is losing its populist appeal and, in the process, becoming a less interesting, less socially and economically diverse place.

At the same time, in Vermont, small villages that have maintained their rural character over the past two centuries have begun falling prey to the same economic forces that are transforming Cambridge. In tiny Belmont, two massive, suburban-style houses built in the last year have single-handedly changed the community's look and feel. Each is several times the size of nearby buildings, and prominently situated, one on a ridge top, the other on a small lake, shattering what was a lovely if unassuming vista of sturdy farmhouses, outbuildings, fields, and the lake. Within the course of a few years, more than two centuries of landscape history – and the pastoral qualities that defined it – have been bulldozed away. They've been replaced by ugly spec-house design, and by enough parking area to fill a small shopping mall. Wither rural Vermont?

What underlies these changes in Cambridge and Belmont is a failure by local communities to anticipate market forces that will invariably bid up and build out real estate in the absence of strong regulatory controls, whether anti-snob zoning or design guidelines. In Cambridge, a strong affordable housing constituency has existed for decades. But hi-tech firms and Harvard University – among other property owners – have made development of such housing a hazardous subject for politicians who would otherwise support an increased supply. Existing inventories of affordable housing in Cambridge hover around the state-mandated minimum of 10 percent; with the abolition of rent control several years ago, this has created a crisis demanding bold action. It would include the adoption of stricter inclusionary zoning measures, requiring private developers to build more affordable units. Passage of the Community Preservation Act (CPA) in Cambridge in 2001 – allowing the city to raise property taxes by up to 3 percent to finance affordable housing, parks, or historic preservation – should help.

Meanwhile, in Vermont, many communities such as Belmont lack any local land use controls. Places under siege from irresponsible development must enact design standards and restrictions on ridge top development, or risk losing a built landscape in keeping with rural culture. Ironically, these are the same places, the same local cultures, that have traditionally been resistant to such regulations in the name of Yankee individualism and independence. Good fences, the quintessential New Englander Robert Frost tells us, make good neighbors, but that's only so long as your neighbors don't build a 10-unit subdivision or 5,000 square foot French-style chateau.

I've had the privilege of living in two disparate but equally distinctive places, and I'm disturbed by their transformation. But my dual domiciles have allowed me to see a common solution, applicable to both cities and rural towns: good zoning rules, grounded in a commitment to preserving the qualities – whether social or scenic – that make a community like no other. Notwithstanding its checkered past and frequent misuse, zoning can be a powerful force for positive change in the life and character of New England's villages and cities. But good zoning rules are not easy to create. Like classic Vermont farmhouses, they are a skilled craft, demanding hard work, care, and, most important, a commitment to place.

The Greening of a Boston Brownfield

The Boston Globe
June 2002

With so much to criticize in President George W. Bush's environmental record, it's a wonder there's anything to applaud.

But there is. The Brownfields Revitalization Act, signed into law earlier this year, eight years after the first brownfields bill was introduced in Congress, authorizes $200 million per year for states, local governments, tribes, and redevelopment authorities for site assessments and cleanups to spur revitalization in communities long scarred by toxic sites.

Perhaps more than any other landscape feature, brownfields are ecology's most powerful emblem of human neglect and shortsightedness. They represent the untoward costs of the American dream, if not its hollow core – the negative social and environmental effects American capitalism has until recently refused to acknowledge, let alone remedy.

Brownfield sites and the pollution that has claimed them are a dual manifestation of an economic system that fails to discriminate between desirable and undesirable costs so long as money changes hands. The gross domestic product, the standard measure of American economic health, thus treats brownfield sites as a multiple economic gain: Money is spent on the industrial production that results in pollution being released into the environment, again when a polluted site is assessed and cleaned up, again when individuals pay for health care, insurance, and other measures to mitigate the pollution's ill effects, and yet again when a new, clean site is developed. This kind of national accounting system makes the recent financial scandals among some of the country's largest corporations pale in comparison.

But brownfields are more than just a symbol of a flawed economic system. They tell us something important about ourselves as a nation.

Brownfields are the byproducts of the wholesale economic disinvestment that followed the flight of white, middle-class families from America's inner cities to the suburbs after World War II. Urban brownfields thus remain as markers of a pervasive social and spatial segregation in which people of color have been confined largely to the nation's urban centers, often next door to brownfield sites, while whites overwhelmingly have populated the significantly less polluted suburbs.

Brownfields are an expression of our civic values and preferences – for a minimalist state, for individualism, for keeping company among our own, for suburbs over cities. Their raw numbers – well over half a million by some estimates – suggest they are not deviations from the norm but the baseline condition, at least in most urban areas. We are a nation of brownfields.

But if brownfields tell a distressing story as symbols of dereliction and despair, then efforts to revitalize them tell an equally powerful tale of uplift. Consider the recent case of 65 Bay St. in Dorchester.

A 4 1/2-acre brownfield just north of Interstate 93, the site was targeted for redevelopment in 1992 by the Dorchester Bay Economic Development Corporation, which eventually purchased it a couple of years later. As owner and developer, the corporation fearlessly forged ahead with the project even though there was no end user lined up, no liability protection for extensive pollution on the site, and inadequate financing.

Five years later, in 1999, still without any commitment from a tenant, let alone full financing, the Economic Development Corporation moved forward with cleanup and construction for a 78,000-square-foot building alongside a restored wetland and green space. After several failed attempts, the corporation finally entered into a lease agreement in 2001 with Spire, a high-tech printing company, with 40 new jobs, tax revenues, and a spruced-up site to show for it. Within a matter of weeks, the company will move in, 10 years after the Economic Development Corporation started working on the site.

The hard-won success in redeveloping the Bay Street site underscores the importance of the new Brownfields Revitalization Act. With more money and more public attention, sites like Bay Street can be revitalized more quickly and in greater numbers, helping not only rebuild blighted areas but changing the economic system that has allowed them to languish in the first place. While these sites will never loom as large as wilderness areas or national parks in our environmental imagination, they are just as important. We all live on Bay Street. These sites are our communities, and tell us as much about who we are as more remote, more majestic places.

An Environmentalist's Axe

Northern Woodlands Magazine
Summer 2002

> "I have read many definitions of what a conservationist
> is, and written not a few myself, but I suspect that
> the best one is written not with a pen, but with
> an axe. It is a matter of what a man thinks about
> while chopping, or while deciding what to chop. A
> conservationist is one who is humbly aware that with
> each stroke he is writing his signature on the face of his
> land."
>
> – Aldo Leopold

When my wife Sally and I bought our farmhouse in
southern Vermont several years ago, the land on which it
sits, 24 acres hard against the Green Mountain National
Forest below a small mountain, had seen better days. Once a
sprawling sheep farm of fields and shade trees, a dense tangle
of third-growth hardwoods and conifers had reclaimed the
site alongside two large tree plantations, one white pine,
the other white spruce. The woods now concealed the old
stone walls, laced with primitive barbed wire, as well as a
host of apple trees and several dilapidated potash ovens still
recognizable amidst the jungle-like understory of striped
maple, ash, and pin cherry. The tree growth was so aggressive,
a white ash had taken root underneath the barn, shooting like
an arrow straight out of what was left of the stone foundation.
Like so many other abandoned farms, the land had gone
untended for nearly half a century, allowing the usual pioneers
– white pine, trembling aspen, pin cherry – to assume their
temporary rule. The vast open expanse of a generation ago
had been reduced to less than an acre. Being city folk from

Cambridge, Massachusetts, Sally and I were looking for not only the peace and quiet of the country, but the sense of space and pastoral views only open fields and meadows can provide.

After we purchased the property, we decided to hire a logger to cut the pine plantation and a couple of additional acres, giving him some marketable timber and us 5 open acres around the house in a simple barter exchange. As a practicing environmentalist and genuine tree hugger (I can often be spotted along with my 4-year old daughter belly up to the bark of an old witness elm in Cambridge, our lips puckered and arms open wide), I was deeply conflicted about the idea of clear-cutting, even if the trees we were removing had either been planted or were very young third-growth. I had seen clear-cuts first-hand: large, menacing swaths in places like Humboldt County, California; smaller ones closer to home, in Shrewsbury. For an environmentalist, there are few phrases as awful as clear-cut. They're fighting words. That I would even contemplate such a thing was heresy.

It wasn't an easy decision. Even harder, however, was the aftermath. I'll never forget the morning I awoke to the sound of chainsaws, having driven up from Cambridge the night before. The loggers had been at work for several days and were nearing the end of the job. I jumped up from the bed, heart in my throat, anxious to see the damage. The place was an unspeakable mess, made impassable by the limbage and debris strewn about like bones in a killing field, more an open grave than open space. I was devastated. What had I done?

And then the rains came. What had been an unusually dry summer turned into a very wet early autumn. The cleared area became a mud-slide, the mountain above our property melting like cheddar cheese down the ravaged slope. The mud was so deep my knee-high Wellington's became useless. There, in the muck, was nature's lesson (pun intended): Don't Mess.

And yet, with the help of winter rye, conservation mix, and

a good growing season, the land was soon reborn, restored to its once and future self as field and meadow. In no time, deer, turkey, fisher, moose and bear had discovered the open setting, much to our delight. This past summer, bluebirds visited one of the boxes I set up. What was once a feeling of horror and self-disgust had become a sense of joy and wonder. But more important than my emotional transformation, my experience in reshaping the landscape brought home an important lesson about living on the land and environmental change. To understand the natural world is to realize that for millennia humans have dramatically altered landscapes and the environment in general. In America, for example, indigenous tribes used fire to clear the forest's understory to promote good hunting grounds while white settlers cut down woodlands for agriculture, built dams for power, and filled wetlands for development. This is not to say such practices were environmentally sound or morally correct. But it does suggest that the trees our loggers cleared were not necessarily more "natural" than the fields they succeeded.

Humans inexorably affect their environment, not merely by perceiving it with our five senses (the "shaping perception," the historian Simon Schama calls it, "that makes the difference between raw matter and landscape"), but by using it to meet society's dual needs of economic production (farms, factories) and social reproduction (houses, schools). Too often, environmentalists and city dwellers like me have romanticized woodlands and wilderness, forgetting that even some of the most remote places have, at one time or another, been indelibly changed by human activity. Indeed, wilderness is itself a human construct, a cultural and legal slogan meant to distinguish the blighted from the pristine, the fallen from the sublime, as much a metaphor as an actual place.

In clearing our few acres and restoring a piece of the property's agricultural past, I like to think we acted responsibly with the axe, as Aldo Leopold might put it. The issue is not whether humans should change or reshape the environment. We always have and always will, as long as we are part of ecosystems. Rather, we are faced with a simple question: What kind of environmental change ought we to produce?

Haunted By Waters

Northern Woodlands Magazine
Spring 2003

> "Eventually, all things merge into one, and a river runs
> through it. . . . I am haunted by waters."
> – Norman MacLean

For four years running we've lost our water supply come
the waning days of summer. When we bought our old
farmhouse several years ago we were told the natural spring
just to the south had never run dry, in nearly 200 years. After
all, the house was basically in a swamp, the catch basin for
run off from Olivia Mountain to the west in the heart of one
of only two snowbelts in Vermont. If it's wet anywhere, it's
here. Just look at the trees: clumps of speckled alder, beebe
willow, balsam fir and tamarack pervade the downsloping
property. In a different life, our house would be a pond.
So I figured that between our location and the site's history,
and the fact that we were only part-time residents, the spring
would provide. I was wrong. Notwithstanding the heavy
rains that inevitably fall during mud season, the wet weeks
of autumn, and even the sky-high snowpack of two winters
ago, with each late summer since 1999, our water supply
has departed in a staccato rhythm of hisses and coughs from
every tap and toilet, startling my 4-year old daughter to tears
and sending us on our way, back to the city, thirsty and a bit
unwashed. There's a drought in New England, and it's big.

The funny thing is, as inconvenient as this situation
is, I'm reluctant to do anything about it. Drilling a well's
expensive in Vermont, where it's not unusual to have to
dig 500 feet or more to find a good seam, and locating a
new, more reliable source seems hopeless. In a world full of

conveniences designed to avoid nature's many vagaries, our fragile water supply is one of the few ways I can connect with the environment, unmediated and uncontrolled.

Living in a modern, post-industrial city like Cambridge, it's hard to experience nature beyond the day's weather. Most of the trees are planted, the rivers channelized and dammed, and the hills chopped down. Aside from a tall drumlin in Mt. Auburn Cemetery, the nation's first urban park, the tallest point in Cambridge is a former landfill. What's more, owing to impervious surfaces like asphalt that cover around 80 percent of the city's surface area, Cambridge has no capacity to store water nature's way, in wetlands, which have all but disappeared. In addition, because urban groundwater is so contaminated, it's not safe for drinking. The environmental laws in Massachusetts, as in most states, accept this as an immutable fact of urban life. As a result, for places like Cambridge, the pollution regulations don't require cleanup of contaminated groundwater, creating a downward spiral of degradation. In a city known for its historic Charles River, a stone's throw from the great Massachusetts Bay, water in Cambridge presents a troubling paradox: it's everywhere, and nowhere, at once exposed and buried by the city's hard surfaces, not a drop to drink.

Our water supply is thus piped in from reservoirs outside the urban edge. Turn on the faucet, and the water's always there. Any time of the year. In rural Vermont, conversely, what you see is what you get. To determine the adequacy of our supply, all I have to do is look at the stream that forms the northern border of our property. If it's low, our supply is low, simple as that. I now find myself looking at rivers and streams with a heightened sense of their importance, and not just as a source of drinking water. As an occasional flyfisherman, I have become acutely aware of just how vulnerable trout and other species are in Vermont's waters. As if sedimentation, eutrophication, invasive species, and other problems weren't enough, Vermont's chronic drought has rendered many of the state's fisheries mere puddles in all but the wettest of times. Whether in town or country, our water resources are distressingly fragile.

Experts on global climate change tell us that extremes in weather – from drought to deluge – will become more common in the years ahead as the planet's ocean currents shift and ambient temperatures rise. Meanwhile, demands on local water supplies from development will become only more problematic in the years ahead as communities begin to bump up against the upper limits of natural systems. In eastern Massachusetts, the lack of water will be the main factor constraining growth in the next 25 years. Out west, many predict suburban Denver will run out of water within a decade.

It's an irony of modern engineering that a person close to a water source can go dry while those in cities, blind to and far removed from the source can have all they want, at least until some government imposes restrictions. Ultimately, urban and rural communities are dependent on the same water systems, but only in the sticks do you really get to know there's a problem. There's no way to conceal it, to engineer it away. The real question is what's worse: Going without water but understanding why, or having plenty but being ignorant?

What Can We Do? A Symposium on Sustaining Nature

Harvard Design Magazine
Spring/Summer 2003

Changing the urban development system in ways that sustain nature and promote livable communities requires working incrementally to demonstrate the benefits of sustainable development and in turn cumulatively transform private markets and public policy into instruments of a sustainable development system. It will not be easy. It will take time, perhaps 50 years, maybe a century. It will be a great struggle, but with great rewards.

By sustainable development, I mean development efforts that attempt to restore environmental quality and eliminate pollution and waste, provide direct, meaningful economic opportunities for all communities, and build civic capacity to plan and manage a healthy future. Such development aims to reinforce a community's unique identity, history, and character, as well as its ecological integrity; it seeks to create places whose walk-ability, human-scale, and usable public spaces, among other assets, help inspire both deeply personal and robustly civic thoughts and feelings. These are places, in the environmental planner Tim Beatley's words, "of enduring value that people are not ashamed to leave to their descendants." Bold aims, I know, but this is an ideal to be pursued, not something we can create overnight.

The key to achieving this kind of development, and to changing the urban development system, are people who are aware of and practice sustainable development methods, like mixed-use, transit-oriented projects of the sort Jane Jacobs advocated over half a century ago, eco-industrial parks that convert one firm's waste into another's energy, urban agriculture, and green buildings, to name a few.

Take community development corporations (CDCs), for instance. The mission of CDCs is to support housing and economic development in distressed communities, where environmental problems such as toxic "brownfield" sites, air pollution, and lead poisoning are commonplace. CDCs share the values of sustainability and are naturally motivated to capture the environmental, public health and financial gains of green design and other sustainable development techniques. Further, through their close community ties and presence throughout the state, CDCs can play a leadership role in raising awareness among a larger public about the benefits and advantages of sustainable development while bringing about local demand for better regulations and public policies. As well, viewed in the aggregate the 65 Massachusetts CDCs, not to mention others around the country, represent an important potential purchaser of sustainable development products and services such as renewable energy and recycled materials.

Through a program called the Green CDCs Initiative, community developers in and around Boston are engaging in sustainable development efforts. In Cambridge, a local CDC developing a 60-unit affordable housing project recently decided to make some design changes to improve the project's environmental performance, including installing pervious parking surface materials to improve drainage and filter run-off, using non-toxic paints and other building matierals, and recycling construction and demolition debris. In Dorchester, another CDC recently completed the largest industrial redevelopment in the state in a decade. The project, a manufacturing facility employing over 140 area residents, was built on a 4-acre brownfield site abutting the Savin Hill T station and next door to a large, very dense residential neighborhood. It includes over an acre of restored greenspace and a wetland. In Boston's Fenway neighborhood, the local CDC has developed a long-term Urban Village Plan to transform the neighborhood from its current conditions – lots of cars and traffic, too many gas stations – to a place where the dominant features will be pedestrians, a vibrant street scene, and the beautiful wetlands for which the neighborhood is named. They're working with local landowners, including the Boston Red Sox, as partners in promoting a human-scale, pedestrian-friendly community.

Meanwhile, private developers are also responding. Working with their industry clients, private developers are becoming leaders in green design and sustainable development as they come to recognize not only the economic and environmental advantages of this approach but improved community relations and a less onerous regulatory process. In Cambridge, one developer, Lyme Properties, is building a mixed-use project on what was formerly an 11-acre brownfield site. The project includes a new bio-tech headquarters building which achieved a "Platinum" rating from the U.S. Green Building Council, making it one of the greenest buildings in the country.

These are examples of real planning and development projects that are changing the way urban developers go about their business. They are also protecting and restoring the urban environment in substantial, though still incremental, ways. But as I said, change will happen slowly, incrementally – one site, one project at a time. It's the cumulative effects of these efforts, over a period of years, that will, I believe, create the feedback loop to policymakers and the private market that will spawn better policies and practices.

A Lesson Before Hiking

Northern Woodlands Magazine
Fall 2003

It seems every year we learn of more weekend warriors going down the primrose path in New England's backcountry. The typical scenario goes something like this: An overeager urban/suburbanite heads out for a strenuous but revitalizing trek or ski in the sublime wilderness. He unknowingly chooses a particularly dangerous and remote route and is equipped with neither the proper experience nor gear to handle the trip. Several hours or a couple of days later he fails to return at the appointed time and an expensive and difficult search ensues. Finally, he emerges, searchers at his side, scathed but smiling, like more than a few skiers and snowboarders this past winter. Alternatively, like the Brooklyn Rabbi who went for a short hike on Franconia Notch in June, 2001, he dies, helpless and alone.

The story of the uninitiated venturing into the wild is at least as old as the nation itself. From the Pilgrims at Plymouth to the Donner Party in the High Sierra, Americans have shown a distinct willingness to risk it all in the wilderness in search of something better. But today's weekend warriors, unlike their counterparts of earlier times, who braved harsh Atlantic voyages and endured hardscrabble lives on farms and in factories, know very little of the perils and challenges, not to mention the expanse, of unsettled terrain.

Today's metropolitan areas offer few opportunities to experience nature in its undomesticated, unengineered state, away from highways, shopping centers, and subdivisions. Most of us have no idea what the country's large, undeveloped woodlands are like: the endless steep and rocky slopes, darkened by a thick canopy of trees; the stream beds cascading every which way; the beaver ponds and meadows, soggy swaths of open space and buzzing flies hinged to the forest's edge. At lower elevations, old stonewalls and logging roads languish in the undergrowth. Higher up, the woods get steeper and denser until the harsh alpine zone, where, surrounded only by sedges, dwarf conifers and rock, one is naked to the frozen wind. It's a far cry from the local park or nature center.

What's more, thanks to modern conveniences like cell phones, global positioning devices, and off-road vehicles, we've been lulled into believing there's no place out of reach, no place we can't get to or find off the beaten path. Ironically, it's this same smug sense that leads too many hikers to go without even the most basic outdoor gear, like sturdy hiking shoes, warm, waterproof clothing, a map, a water bottle, a knife, a whistle.

Lost weekend hikers and skiers are more than just an object lesson in the importance of being prepared. They are a parable of a lost, denatured society, one that has come to believe that driving an SUV is tantamount to living off the land, that survival means nothing more than what we can watch on a television show in the comfort of our living rooms. Removed from any meaningful connection to undeveloped, unforgiving places, we've lost touch with what it means to be alone on this earth, the vulnerable creatures that we are.

A variety of outdoor programs are available to acquaint people of all ages and abilities with the rigors and hazards, as well as the sublime beauty, of wilderness so they can learn more fully to understand and respect these places. But more important than wilderness education, we should more aggressively protect and restore large, wild places in our metropolitan areas, like Forest Park in Portland, Oregon, the San Francisco Bay Area's Marin Headlands, the "urban wilds" of New York City's Jamaica Bay, or the great stretch of pine barrens just 30 miles outside Boston in southeastern Massachusetts, to ensure ready access to undomesticated nature. Perhaps only when the city and countryside are more closely aligned, in a less developed, more rugged landscape, will we finally find ourselves, a bit less accommodated, but certainly more alive.

Farewell to 'the People's Republic'

The Boston Globe
June 2004

"A place is a piece of the whole environment that has been claimed by feelings," my neighbor's brother, an environmental philosopher, writes. As I prepare to depart the city of Cambridge, where I've lived and worked for over a decade, I'm drawn to these words as I reflect on the place and people I'm leaving.

I arrived in Cambridge from Berkeley on a sweltering July afternoon in 1993. Rent control was still in effect and the high-tech bubble that would emerge later in the '90s, fundamentally changing this and so many other cities, was still a technologist's pipe dream.

With a new administration in the White House, there was a buzz about town, a sense of hope and possibility. The People's Republic of Cambridge was alive and kicking. I came to the area to launch a non-profit agency and to teach at Boston College Law School. I was, and remain, a social entrepreneur, committed to helping solve entrenched problems like environmental degradation in inner-city neighborhoods. Given the region's rich stock of nonprofit organizations and academic resources, Cambridge was the perfect place to be, a city of dreamers.

What a difference a decade makes. Whereas 10 years ago someone in their 20s making a modest nonprofit salary could afford to live in Cambridge, today it's no longer possible. For most nonprofit professionals and academics, not to mention others earning less than six figures, Cambridge is simply off-limits as a place to live and raise a family.

The modest condominium my wife and I stretched to afford in 1996 we sold eight years later for more than twice what we paid for it. It's no accident that the purchaser was a young mutual fund executive. Who else but a money manager could afford to buy in Cambridge?

The problem is, Cambridge appears to be losing the very qualities that have made it unique, a haven for idealists and rebels, for thinkers and writers, for iconoclasts and visionaries, jobs that tend not to command much compensation. With more million-dollar houses than any other comparable city in the country, Cambridge can no longer rightfully be called "the People's Republic." It's an anachronism.

I think for many who live in Cambridge what keeps them here is precisely this mix of characters, this openness to different ways of looking at the world and embrace of contrarian attitudes and ideologies. Yet now, like the fragile floodplain it once was, attracting all manner of wildlife and waterfowl, Cambridge finds itself threatened by the market's unmitigated forces and the cash of the highest bidder. Social activists need not apply.

As my family and I pack up our belongings to head for an old farmhouse in Vermont, I leave Cambridge knowing that my feelings have claimed this place, and been claimed by it – by its root-buckled sidewalks and triple-deckers, the rumble of the T underfoot in Central Square, the annual rite of students receiving their diplomas then moving on, the perfect foil for us, the proud assemblage of full-timers who love this city because it's not fly-by-night but enduring in its rebellious spirit and diversity.

Still I wonder: Is Cambridge becoming less of a place and more of an idea of a place, of something that once was but is no longer? I'm not sure. But I hope that somehow Cambridge finds a way to hold onto its dreamers and agitators, its philosophers and folk singers. The city needs them. So does the world.

Who Governs the Forest?

Northern Woodlands Magazine
Fall 2004

I was recently in Colorado meeting with a group of civic
leaders, environmentalists, geographers, and planners from
across the Rocky Mountain states to discuss the future of
landscape conservation across the region. As an easterner, an
outsider, I was struck by two basic facts of western life: First,
unlike the Northeast, the Rocky Mountain west is dominated
by the presence of public lands. They're everywhere. Over 80
percent of Nevada's land area is publicly owned; public lands
account for over 60 percent of Utah and Idaho.

Second, as my friend Dan Kemmis, director of the Center
for the Rocky Mountain West, described at our meeting,
westerners feel a certain ownership over these national lands
owing to their proximity to and dependence on them.
They are not abstract national treasures; they are backyards,
viewsheds, and the building blocks of local economies.
Because of this, Dan urges federal agencies to give more
decision-making power to local groups of resource users,
environmentalists, and business owners over managing and
using public lands, to give them priority, in a sense, over other
taxpayers. This locally driven, collaborative process, Dan
suggests, can help ameliorate the rancor and polarization that
has for decades characterized western lands policy.

Now, listening to Dan I was reminded of the fact that,
like the westerners Dan is concerned about, I live surrounded
by public lands, in my case, the Green Mountain National
Forest. I'm an inholder and each day when I walk out my
door am greeted by the pay-off of decades' worth of public
investment: maturing forestlands, wetlands teeming with
life, rich stocks of wildlife like moose and bear. I feel a deep

connection to these lands, this place, a sense of ownership that is moral far more than monetary.

Then, come winter, I hear the drone of snowmobiles on the network of trails that snakes through our part of the national forest, not unbearable, but a nuisance. Many of the riders aren't from around here; they're outsiders, visitors, like I was when I lived in the city and came up on weekends. Eventually I settle myself with the idea that this land is their land, too. Easy to say, tougher to internalize.

The debate over our national forests, it seems to me, boils down to a straightforward but complex question: Should some publics be considered more important than others for the purposes of public lands management? That is, should people who live in or near public lands – "communities of place" who derive their livelihoods and sense of identity from these resources – be entitled to a greater say than outsiders – "communities of interest," who value the non-economic benefits of public lands but live far away – over how they're used?

For those of us who live at some remove from our national forests and wilderness areas, whether we're in cities or in states with few large tracts of publicly owned land, it's easy to see these public assets through a tourist's lens. We can appreciate the beauty and power of these places but we're not around long enough to really get to know them or the people whose livelihoods are intermingled with them – the loggers, miners, park rangers, motel owners, and others who call our public lands home.

The city dweller in me wants to assert my interest regardless of my place. Public land, after all, is as much mine as it is yours. But the inholder in me says, "Wait a minute." It seems to me what really matters is not where I live nor what my interest is, but two other issues at the core of a good society – accountability and adaptability.

People who make decisions about how to manage public lands should first and foremost be accountable for the consequences of those decisions, whether they're local groups or remote lawgivers. They should be accountable for educating themselves and the public at large about the key issues at stake in managing public lands – environmental, economic, and otherwise – and making the difficult trade-offs between them.

Which leads to the importance of adaptability. We must be able to revise our public lands decisions in light of new and better understandings about not only healthy ecosystems but also the people and economies whose own health derives from them. This "adaptive management" approach is our best hedge against bad decisions and the political and ecological complexity inherent in all public lands policy.

Whether we live in Vermont or Colorado, in a national forest or hundreds of miles away, these two principles should be constant. Would that it were so.

Fall Forest

Vermont Public Radio
October 2004

The fall's a funny time of year around here, what with all the tour buses and SUVs full of leaf peepers drawn like moths to the candy-colored foliage of maples, birches, and ash. As a former part-time Vermonter, I get it. I mean, what's not to love about the northern forest in autumn, the ocean of reds and golds, oranges and yellows. It sure beats your average street tree or the duller hues of the transition forest farther to the south where I used to live.

As I've come to spend more time in Vermont and know the forest better, I look at the fall differently. For me, it's not about the golds or yellows anymore, not about the maples or birches.

There's a balsam fir, two actually, that stand alongside an alder swamp on the west side of our property. In the summer, they're completely hidden by the hardwoods nearby; the firs' short needles and spiky silhouette are no match for the birches wide-spreading branches or the ash's towering height. If you didn't know better, you'd think there were no conifers over there.

But then, in mid-September, about the time I start closing my windows at night, something magical happens. As the leaves change color, the fir trees begin to appear as if in bold relief, their delicate green the perfect contrast to the gaudy yellows and oranges. For me, autumn is the time when I'm reminded about what makes the green mountains green. Sure, in the summer, the whole forest is verdant; but in the fall, and then the winter, even into spring, it's the conifers – the spruce and fir – that define our mountain zone, that separate our woods from their more temperate cousins found at lower elevations and points south.

When I rediscover my fir trees each fall I rediscover not what drew me to this state but what keeps me here. It's not about the colors but the hills, the hardiness and humility that come from living with long winters and a short growing season. It's about a landscape that's beautiful not because it's more vast or spectacular than any other but because it's time-tested, enduring, and, like my fir trees, elegant in its understated power.

So let's celebrate the foliage season with its autumnal glow and bright palette. But not too much. After all, as our Vermont friend Robert Frost warns us, "nothing gold can stay." I think the green is gold. It's what remains after the visitors have gone, after the glow has faded to gray. And in case you forgot, November is right around the corner.

Mountains and Mileage

Northern Woodlands Magazine
Winter 2005

My driver's license was suspended for ten days in December. I racked up 10 points for speeding, twice in the same spot on Route 7 just south of Danby. In 24 years of driving, I probably got less than ten tickets, total. Last year alone, I was tagged with three.

As a relative newcomer to Vermont, having lived most of my life in cities, I'm not used to driving as much and as far as I do now. For the past dozen years I lived in Cambridge, Massachusetts, one of the most densely settled places on earth, not far behind Hong Kong in the number of residents per square mile. In cities like Cambridge, you can walk, bike, or take a train almost anywhere; a car is optional.

But in southern Vermont, where the National Forest dominates, with its many summits, valleys and slopes, getting from point A to point B isn't so easy. It's one of the great ironies of rural life. Those of us who live "close to the land," where natural areas are still largely in tact, have to spend a lot of time in gas-guzzling cars and trucks owing to nature's very presence. Meanwhile, in cities, where finding even the barest signs of indigenous nature can sometimes be hard, folks can generally move around in much more environmentally benign ways.

The lesson here is that cities aren't as unfriendly to nature as they appear to be, nor are rural places like Vermont as environmentally virtuous as we in the Green Mountain State would like to believe. In other words, cities and countryside each possess their own unique advantages and disadvantages when it comes to environmental responsibility. And therein lies an opportunity for learning.

Cities teach us that density – living close to eachother – can be a good thing. It's what brings people out of their living rooms and onto the street: for a walk, to say Hello to a neighbor, or just to sit on a stoop and observe life's daily grind. Whether in Cambridge or one of Vermont's countless village centers, density is the glue that binds a community, that creates its vital core while allowing mobility that's not car-dependent.

Rural areas – defined by their lack of dense settlement – remind us that our ability to experience nature in its unengineered state – free of streetlights or sidewalks or exotic plantings – is itself a benefit. Not only do healthy forests and wetlands provide essential services like clean air and clean water, but they also supply recreational and spiritual amenities – trails for hiking and skiing, streams for swimming and fishing, and scenery for inspiration and repose.

As technology, population, and other forces continue to reshape Vermont's landscape, we must be mindful of how our settlement patterns affect our environment. While there will likely never be a light rail system shuttling commuters in southern Vermont, I sure hope we encourage more urban-style development in our downtowns: greater density, less parking lots, more sidewalks. At the same time, we need to make sure our vast expanse of forest remains green: fewer ridge top mansions (but perhaps more ridge top wind turbines, an environmentally correct way of off-setting some of the greenhouse gases we produce from all our driving), less pavement, no cul-de-sacs.

I guess part of living in Vermont, and in rural places generally, is not only accepting but embracing the slower pace of things, not so much in terms of the quaintness of country life but in the absolute sense: living in Vermont simply isn't as fast-paced as in other, more urban places. In the absence of big-city hustle and bustle, we're afforded one of life's true luxuries – the opportunity to look around, to be present, to experience, and not merely be governed by, the passage of time.

Perhaps my speeding tickets were thus a kind of (traffic) signal telling me not just to slow down but to appreciate life as it's happening around me: on the road, at home, in the office. Urban or rural, the point's the same. Oh yea, and one more thing: Cruise control is my new best friend.

A Republic of Trees

Vermont Public Radio
April 2005

Trees are nature's superlatives. The oldest living thing on the planet is a bristle cone pine, 5000 years old and still extant in the American southwest. California's coast redwood is the tallest, rising a vertiginous 380 feet above the forest floor. Among the largest living things – a stand of aspen, acres of roots comprising a single living system.

In Vermont, spring time reminds me of our own super trees. Though much of Vermont's woodlands have yet to leaf out, there's something about them in early spring that stops me in my muddy tracks. Unlike the monumental trees of the west, our trees are notable less as individual star species than a remarkable supporting cast. Take the paper birch with its chalky bark luffing in the wind, like a white flag of truce after the long, harsh winter. Or the sugar maples festooned with sap buckets at the skirt, giving of their sweet life-blood to the new season. There's the occasional basswood, the stout edge-dweller of old farmfields with its broad crown and brittle limbs. And don't forget the ubiquitous white pine, the consummate pioneer ever on the prowl for the warm spring sun.

The list goes on. The apple and ash, beech and butternut, spruce and shadbush. What we lack in star-power we make up for with variety and sheer quantity. But in the early spring, you have to work hard to distinguish one tree from the next. From a distance, especially in the mountains, Vermont's woodlands appear colorless, a stark contrast to autumn. Without leaves, they are naked and wan.

Many have been diminished by winter's fierce winds and temperatures. Were it not for the fringe of spruce and fir at elevation, or the backdrop of a blue sky, I wonder if people would even notice the forest this time of year. It's a shadow presence.

But it's precisely this unassuming quality that makes Vermont's trees so compelling in April. They are a paradox, at once inconspicuous and totally dominating. Without snow or the green grass of summer, April's trees are all we've got. They literally hold the landscape together, what with the run-off from the snow melt and rain which, without them, would cause Vermont simply to ooze away.

As I walk the trails behind our house, I realize that in this naked season I feel most connected to the forest. There's nothing to distract me, my feet penetrating the damp soil and touching the tangled roots, as if connecting me to the very heartwood of every tree in the forest. It's now, in April, when I realize that Vermont is as much a republic of trees as it is of people, that it's the collective, not the individual, that matters, the connection of one thing to another holding it all together.

Trout Nation

Vermont Public Radio
June 2005

I recently stocked my pond with a few dozen trout. I got them from Matt Daneher, an energetic man whose hobby is raising thousands of trout of all shapes and sizes in a bunch of holding ponds around his North Shrewsbury property.

This was my first trip to a hatchery. An occasional flyfisherman, and not a very good one at that, I figured my best chance of catching a Vermont trout would be from my own pond. I've been fishing southern Vermont's waters for years but with little to show for it save for a few small brook trout and one big brown I caught with a guide on the Black River back in 2002. A couple of Sundays ago I headed down to Vermont's signature trout stream, the Battenkill, to try my luck. Though I've fished the Battenkill almost a dozen times, I've yet to catch a single fish.

Like I said, I'm not much of an angler, but it seems I'm not alone in finding Vermont's streams particularly unyielding. An Orvis guide told me that he doesn't even fish the Vermont portion of the Battenkill anymore. Today, he reports, there are less than 100 trout per stream mile, as compared to over 1400 as recently as 1992. On-going studies by the Vermont Fish and Wildlife Department suggest that one factor might be streambank erosion, which is burying the fish's breeding grounds, resulting in a shrinking wild brown trout population. Another factor appears to be degraded water quality from nutrients and other pollutants entering the stream. Trout are sensitive to even small changes in water quality.

Like the great salmon of the Pacific Northwest whose dramatic decline has led to a call for the restoration of

"Salmon Nation," Vermont's trout are symbolic species, indicators of not just the health of our rivers and watersheds but the region's history and culture. Perhaps in Vermont we should consider promoting the slogan "Trout Nation," at least in the Battenkill watershed.

Last weekend, I headed to a nearby lake with my fly rod. I figured if I can't catch trout, small mouth bass will have to do. While approaching the lake in my pick up truck I noticed a large bird perched on a boulder at the water's edge. Given its size, I immediately stopped my truck and got out to look more closely. There, in the glitter of a sunny Saturday morning, was a rare sight: a lone Bald Eagle, his iconic white hood and tail feathers in impressive display as he quickly took flight. Not so long ago you couldn't see a Bald Eagle in these parts. The eagle reminded me of nature's resilience and of the fact that with awareness and care, we can help restore what we've damaged.

Later, as I drove away, still considering the plight of Vermont's native trout, I found myself thinking of that Emily Dickinson poem. It must have been the eagle, because it was the one that begins, "Hope is a thing with feathers."

From New Orleans to a Better Future

Vermont Public Radio
September 2005

On a radio talk show the other night, a New Orleans journalist, commenting on the city's resilience and pride in the face of Hurricane Katrina's devastation, sounded a defiant tone. He said that within a matter of months the city would rebuild its broken levies and buildings and return to normal. One would expect such comments from a survivor. But what was really striking was what the journalist didn't say. He failed to note that the Federal Emergency Management Agency warned in 2001 that a hurricane striking New Orleans was one of the three most likely disasters in the U.S, or that a year later, the New Orleans Times-Picayune published a five-part series predicting that the city would one day be flooded by even a relatively mild hurricane once its levees were breached. The series' authors argued for an immediate shift in development and environmental policies so as to avoid the building patterns that left the area ever more vulnerable to disaster.

Equally troubling, the journalist made no mention of the fact that the overwhelming majority of Katrina's victims so far have been the city's blacks and low-income residents. Katrina, like so many other so-called "natural disasters," is really a poor person's catastrophe: those with the fewest resources suffer the most. In New Orleans, a city precariously situated below Lake Pontchartrain and the Mississippi River on unstable marshes, low-income residents live in the lowest of the bottomlands, putting them at greatest risk of flooding and related hazards. The journalist's omissions speak volumes about a problem not only in New Orleans but across the nation's cities and towns: our collective unwillingness to plan for and invest in development that both sustains our essential natural systems and ensures our most vulnerable populations are not left behind. For three centuries, Americans have found a way to bulldoze, backfill and otherwise engineer our way around many of nature's obstacles – from tidelands to fire zones to fault lines. Invariably, these fixes have proved temporary, if not outright foolhardy.

At the same time, through a combination of public policy and market decisions, we've made sure that people of color and low-income residents are left with the least desirable parts of our cities and towns – the flood-prone Mill Creek area of West Philadelphia, Oakland's noisy highway corridors, the blighted industrial zones of East St. Louis, Los Angeles's abandoned oil fields.

Frederich Engels warned that "In nature, nothing takes place in isolation. . . . Each conquest" he said, "takes its revenge on us." He was right. New Orleans's failure to pursue a path of more sustainable and equitable development has affected all of us – at the gas pump, in the halls of Congress and, perhaps most importantly, in our hearts. We owe it to Katrina's victims, to the city of New Orleans and to the nation as a whole to heed the lessons from this experience and begin to make better choices about how and where we live.

Toll Brothers

Perspectives on Place Blog
October 2005

No sooner had I started to think about our first *Perspectives* entry than the *New York Times* came through with some delicious food for thought. The cover story of the October 16 issue of the Magazine features, of all things, land use and development, in this case the nation's largest home builder, Toll Brothers, and their massive land acquisition efforts over the last decade (Toll Bros. has banked enough land for 80,000 large, new homes).

When was the last time a major news magazine had a cover story about a developer and land development. For me, it's a signal that land use, and its close cousin real estate development, have arrived as major cultural, economic and environmental issues.

A number of items in the piece stand out as particularly relevant to the Foundation's work: (a) Toll Brothers use of *Google Earth* to identify new sites for their land acquisition program. It's a high-profile example of how this new, easily downloadable technology, akin to the Foundation's CommunityViz tool, can be used in the planning and development arena, in this case for commercial purposes; (b) Bob Yaro's comments on the need and prospects for regional governance, to counter the damage done by local land use and development decisions, which tend to simply push off their negative costs on other communities. Yaro's a consistent voice for reason and regionalism in planning amidst the background noise of short-sighted municipalities and reluctant state governments; (c) The comments of Toll Brothers CEO, Bob Toll, on the primacy of NIMBY to their business model and the (dim) prospects for regional governance. NIMBY is a reality, for good or ill. Toll's view: Deal with it; (d) Toll's comments on the importance of local authority as almost an American birthright. Local politics matter when it comes to land use and development, and that's as it should be, and; (e) The positive correlation between stricter zoning and high housing costs. Simple supply and demand.

Interestingly, the same Sunday *Times* included a story in the Real Estate section on a New Urbanist-style development in Georgia, called Serenbe, combining density and open space largely for second-home buyers fleeing Atlanta's congestion and sprawl. The project's 224 acres contain 224 units, with 70 percent open space.

Add these two stories to the KB Homes announcement a week earlier about their partnership with Martha Stewart and you have to wonder if something's in the (land use planning) air.

Seems to me we should all be paying attention to these stories. For example, Bob Toll and his associates are probably more knowledgeable about what land is available in your community and how it's zoned than you are, not to mention your local planning commission. As citizens and planners, we need to be proactive, like Toll Bros., anticipate the growth and other trends that are coming our way, as they are doing, have a 20-year plan, like they have, use the latest tools available e.g., *Google Earth*, like they are doing. Why should real estate development be a more exact science than land use planning? We need to take a page from their playbook and bring as much focus (and resources) to our lands and land uses as they are. Otherwise, companies like Toll Bros. will, de facto, become both the planners and the developers of our communities.

The key going forward is just that: to go forward, to think

ahead, to anticipate and affirm the future we want rather than simply let it come to us.

Toll Bros. has a vision of the future, it's called a business plan, and they are working aggressively to realize that vision. In a sense, communities need business plans, something that gets beyond the platitudes that you mention and gets down to the brass tacks of how we get from here to there. This is what zoning rules and other regulations are supposed to do: implement the vision. But to the extent that they are often proscriptive and negative in nature ("here's what you can't do"), as opposed to enabling ("this is what we want"), they tend to function not so much as instruments of intentional communities but bulwarks of the status quo.

Zoning, if reconceived, can be a creative and positive force in the life of communities; it can be an enabling tool for realizing a common vision and help communities get from where they are to where they want to be. The idea that zoning is inherently bad is an ideology, not a fact. It can be as good, or as bad, as communities choose to make it.

And as any good developer will tell you, when communities come to the table prepared to say exactly what they want, and enshrine that in their local rules, a good developer will respond in kind.

North Woods

Perspectives on Place Blog
November 2005

The North Woods are for sale, or at least 426,000 acres of them. In March, the Seattle-based Plum Timber Company announced plans to develop the largest subdivision in Maine's history: 1000 houses and two resorts in the Moosehead Lake region. Many environmentalists and some state officials fear that the area's rugged beauty will be irreparably harmed by the project, with sprawl and pollution its inevitable effects.

The company, which plans to build the project in phases over 10 years, is promising to set aside 55 lakes as conservation areas, create affordable housing and a business district, provide a permanent 74-mile snowmobile trail and 55 miles of hiking trails and maintain most of the land as a working forest for at least 30 years. In all, only three percent of the developable land will be affected.

More than a six hour drive from the Boston area, the proposed Plum Timber subdivision is the newest and wildest frontier in the land rush that has been gathering steam across New England for the last decade. With coastal real estate now essentially beyond the means of most first and second-home buyers, it was only a matter of time before eager developers and savvy land owners figured it out. I'm surprised it took them so long.

I recall my own situation over a decade ago. Living in Cambridge, Massachusetts, in a modest-sized condominium, my future wife and I had just gotten engaged. Instead of paying for a wedding, we decided to use the funds as a down-payment on a second-home. My wife wanted a beach house, preferably in Maine. I was committed to a Vermont location. It wasn't even close.

The cost difference between coastal and upland real estate, then as now, was substantial, a factor of at least two. The coast was far more than our modest down-payment could afford. It was the mountains or nothing, so we headed north to Vermont and never looked back. We now live in the Green Mountain State full-time.

Today, inland properties are surging in value at an unprecedented rate. And coastal properties? Forget it. Anything on the ocean within a 3-4 hour drive from New York or Boston is now squarely on the Gold Coast. Supply and demand will out.

The Plum Creek proposal is a signal event in the history of New England land use. Thanks to Maine's mix of large coastal and woodland areas, and the remoteness of its eastern and northern sections, the state offers a look at the far-edges of development pressures and patterns. No other New England state even comes close. And what do we see?

The Plum Creek project is an example of what planners call "amenity migration": the movement of people to places that are attractive for non-economic reasons, such as recreation and scenic beauty. Since the 1970s, a growing number of urban dwellers have moved to non-metropolitan amenity destinations, reversing a trend of migration from the country to the city that started in the mid-nineteenth century. In the American West, amenity migration has become one of the largest drivers of economic activity, replacing traditional natural resource extraction industries like mining and logging, which have declined in recent years, as a dominant economic development strategy.

Owing to their scale, ruggedness and off-the-grid location, the North Woods are New England's ultimate amenity destination whose time, it appears, has come, thanks largely to the rapid rise in property values in less remote areas of the region and the inability or unwillingness of a conservation buyer to intervene in the transaction (the state of Maine had already committed to other major land deals in the last few years). The important issue, then, is not whether development can or should happen in the North Woods, as some environmentalists would frame it. It's happening. The real rub is how such development will proceed – haphazardly, carelessly and irresponsibly, or deliberately, creatively and with the region's special ecological and cultural qualities in mind.

From the looks of it, Plum Creek seems committed to the latter approach, with its promises to conserve land, provide affordable housing, promote tourism and economic development and maintain a working forest. As more timber companies like Plum Creek, which is structured as a real estate investment trust, move out of the resource extraction business and into real estate development, and as amenity destinations continue to attract an increasingly mobile and flexible population, the key is that environmentalists, local businesses, state and local officials and residents join developers in planning and implementing projects that strike the right balance between environmental, economic and social goals. Not an easy task, but is there really any other way?

Wildlife in Cities

Perspectives on Place Blog
May 2006

In "Unto the City the Wildlife Did Journey," Andy Newman writes in the *New York Times* that "Bears, a moose, a coyote and other animals have visited the New York area, and a fair degree of chaos has ensued." Another illustration of cities becoming more "rural" (wildlife) while rural areas and exurbs become more urban (housing, people, etc.). More people are moving out from our central cities and suburbs to find cheaper housing and a better quality of life, trading mortgage sticker-shock for 2 hour commutes (one-way!), while businesses go in search of the same under the banner "location-neutrality." In some cases, the two are one and the same, no commute necessary.

Wall Street in the woods of Litchfield County. Farmers markets in Union Square. Artist lofts in old mill towns like Easthampton, Massachusetts. Seals off Staten Island.

The puzzle pieces are starting to create an interesting picture. Urban-rural, rural-urban: We're fast becoming one continuous geography, a seamless web of wildlife, Wi-Fi and .
. . .

Vermont Must Conserve Its Human Resources

Burlington Free Press
June 2006

Demographers are telling us that Vermont will soon have the second oldest population behind Maine, having lost roughly twenty percent of our twenty to thirty-four year-olds – twice the national average – in the last decade. Meanwhile, our workforce is shrinking and three quarters of our public schools have seen their enrollments decline since 2000.

I think what the demographers are really saying is that Vermonters need to begin to reimagine our economic and social policies if we want to have a future with more than just a few people in it. Perhaps we don't, and would prefer to see Vermont the state replaced by Vermont the park, a continuous stretch of forest and farmland from Pownal to Peacham, flanked by Burlington and a scattering of gateway communities for tourists, telecommuters and those fortunate enough to make a living from their knowledge or their land.

If we want Vermont the state, however, it starts with a new vision, a twenty-first century approach that borrows from the best thinking in community development and civic renewal. There's no magic involved, just the political will to do a number of things simultaneously, like invest in affordable housing, in downtown revitalization, in workforce development and in hi-tech infrastructure, measures that balance the desire to protect small town character and scenic landscapes with the imperative of attracting the young families and workers who comprise Vermont's future generations.

A new vision for Vermont would build on the state's recently enacted Growth Centers bill and the tried-and-true work of the Vermont Housing and Conservation Board by creating a bold enterprise program to seed and support small to mid-size businesses from agriculture to green technology to internet retail. It would seek to recruit new immigrant communities who bring entrepreneurial energies and a strong work ethic and, in turn, help attract younger residents increasingly accustomed to cultural diversity and its myriad social benefits.

Next, we need to elevate our bedrock environmental law, Act 250, by making it Vermont's human resources statute, its magnet for luring the developers and businesses who understand the relationship between quality development and quality of life. We need to compliment the Act's emphasis on regulation with incentives like a green development fund and location efficiency credits to encourage sound land use decisions – for example, building affordable, energy-efficient modular townhouses near schools, stores and employment centers.

The environmentalist David Brower once said about pessimism, "It's a luxury we can no longer afford." I like to think about Vermont's population estimates in the same spirit, as an opportunity disguised as something else. If we look at it this way, then no matter what the demographers say, the future looks bright.

Poetic Communities

Vermont Public Radio
September 2006

"To fail as a poet," the philosopher Richard Rorty tells us, "is to accept somebody else's description of oneself, to execute a previously prepared program, to write, at most, elegant variations on previously written poems." For Rorty, a poet isn't just someone who writes verse; she's anyone who strives for invention, who finds the old ways inadequate to deal with new experiences.

Given this definition, Sigmund Freud was a poet because he changed our map of the mind by creating a new vocabulary that combined economics with legends and myths. George Orwell was a poet, too. He redescribed communism in the colorful, if radical, terms of allegory, leaving the world to behold a once grand notion turned poisonous.

But poets need not be great thinkers or novelists. They need not even be individuals. Take the small town of Wray, Colorado, for example, on the western fringe of the Great Plains. Like many rural Plains communities, Wray sits on a fault line of drought and depopulation. In some ways, Wray still resembles the 19th century frontier town it once was – dry and dusty, with a mere 6 people per square mile in the surrounding area.

But the people of Wray weren't satisfied with simply reprising the same old patterns. They came up with a new vision and a new approach to getting there. When they looked out across the landscape of eastern Colorado, Wray didn't see hardship but promise, in the crops the farmers struggle to grow, the wind that constantly buffets them, the sun that constantly parches them and the local school that, more than any history book, tells the true story of the town

– as it is today and might be tomorrow.

Under the radar, Wray is becoming a model for rural community development in which agriculture and energy production are the starting point for positive change, the preface to a new story of the Great Plains. The local high school has erected a wind turbine to power the school's facilities while educating Wray's younger generation about the possibilities of renewable energy as a source of community renewal. Local farmers and ranchers have come together around ethanol, biomass, methane, wind and solar to help achieve energy independence, not only for Wray but the nation as a whole. And they've helped create 25x25, a national effort to provide 25 percent of the nation's energy needs from U.S. farms, forests and ranches by 2025.

Wray's innovation has begun to turn a story of despair into a story of hope. It's emerging as a symbol of a new, forward-looking rural America. Call it a "poetic community." And there are others – like Paonia, Colorado; Missoula, Montana; Northampton, Massachusetts, and Brattleboro, Vermont. These are places that simply refuse to accept somebody else's definition of what's possible.

I believe in each of us, in each of our communities, is a poet waiting to rise up, and that now, more than ever, we need our poets. So like a preacher, I say, "All rise."

Green Technology Age

Vermont Public Radio
January 2007

It was great to hear Governor Douglas herald the dawn of Vermont's green technology age in his recent inaugural address. Alongside his promise of broadband access for all Vermonters, Douglas has made recruiting environmental businesses a priority.

This is welcome news. But it's also surprising, coming from a Governor who has unconditionally opposed the development of commercial-scale wind facilities in Vermont. Douglas thinks such facilities would "industrialize" Vermont's landscape, out of keeping with the state's rural heritage.

But theses kinds of comments only reinforce an old, and increasingly unhelpful, mental model, in which industrial development is pitted against environmental responsibility.

As advances in green technologies have shown, industry has created some of today's most environmentally beneficial, and aesthetically beautiful, products and places. Think of Toyota's sleek hybrid vehicle, the Prius, or the simple elegance of a solar panel on a farmhouse rooftop, or the Ford Motor Company's new River Rouge manufacturing facility, where the water coming out of the plant is cleaner than the water going in, or UVM's new Davis Center, a model of green design. These are all symbols of an industrialized landscape.

What's more, these innovations are greener in spades than many of the activities and features we associate with Vermont's traditional landscape. Pesticide-dependent agriculture, houses and businesses that rely on oil and gas for heat, ski areas that drink up Vermont's water resources, the nuclear energy supplying a third of the state's electricity, to say nothing of the soot-belching timber mills that dotted

Vermont's woodlands into the twentieth century, their feedstock the clear-cut hillsides that today, regrown with trees, hide their dirty tracks. The counterpart to an industrialized landscape is not necessarily pristine by any stretch.

Meanwhile, without saying so, the Governor is proposing the most ambitious industrial project in Vermont's history in his push for broadband access for every nook and cranny of the state by 2010. This policy amounts to an unprecedented construction boom of satellite dishes, cell towers and fiber optic cable. It also means something else, something more subtle than a satellite dish. Within a few years, there will likely be no spot in Vermont unreachable by a cell phone. For wilderness advocates and true traditionalists, this is a deeply troubling notion, the ultimate industrial accident.

For too long, people have believed that the environments most worth saving are remote, rural places, sparsely settled if at all, and devoid of industry or urbanization. This has resulted in a false choice between, on the one hand, the pristine and on the other, the industrialized. But nature is more complicated than that.

If we are going to live responsibly in Vermont into the future, we must learn to create a new rhetoric and new landscape somewhere between the pristine and the fallen. Whether it's broadband access or wind energy, Vermont will need to change to accommodate the uses and technologies necessary to sustain our society. The result can still be beautiful and clean, but in a different, more human, way.

Foreword to *New Geographies of the American West: Land Use and the Changing Patterns of Place*

Island Press 2007

> There shall be sang another golden age,
> The rise of Empire and the arts
> The good and great inspiring epic sage,
> The wisest heads and noblest hearts.
>
> Not such as Europe breeds in her decay;
> Such as she bred when fresh and young,
> When heavenly flame did animate her clay,
> By future poets shall be sung.
>
> Westward the course of empire takes its way;
> The four first acts already past,
> A fifth shall close the drama with the day;
> Time's noblest offspring is the last.

George Berkeley
Verses on the Prospect of Planting Arts and Sciences in America
(1726)

It was the Vermonter Frederick Billings who, having left New England in the 1840s to seek his fortune in California as a real estate lawyer, financier and railroad entrepreneur, purchased 1200 acres in the East Bay, across from the fast-growing city of San Francisco. With one western town already named after him in Montana, he determined that, rather than call his holding Billingsbroke, as had been suggested by his marketing-savvy peers, he would name it Berkeley, believing that Bishop Berkeley's prophecy of a new Golden Age would take its firmest root in the American West.

The promise of the New World has always found its boldest expression in the West. Beginning with Thomas Jefferson, whose interest in western settlement as a central means for promoting agrarian republicanism inspired the Louisiana Purchase and Corps of Discovery expedition, post-Colonial Americans, seasoned by the East's thick forests and rocky soils, looked beyond their stone walls and cedar fences and fixed their gaze westward in search of land, economic opportunity and the realization of the then still emergent American dream. At mid-century, President James K. Polk refashioned Jefferson's western policy into his doctrine of Manifest Destiny, asserting the necessity and rectitude of American expansionism. Later, the historian Frederick Jackson Turner argued in 1893 in his famous "Frontier Thesis" that America's political success – its democratic institutions and civil liberties – depended upon the rugged individualism forged by the West's frontier experience.

More recently, the writer Wallace Stegner, in his collection *Where the Bluebird Sings to the Lemonade Springs*, bestowed to the West one of its most celebrated passages when he described the region as "hope's native home, the youngest and freshest of America's regions, magnificently endowed and with the chance to become something unprecedented and unmatched in the world." Though he would at times repudiate the idea of the West as the "Geography of Hope," believing that certain regional trends like water policy spelled the West's doom, nevertheless Stegner tapped into a deep cultural vein, one that continues to this day to draw all manner of migrants to the region.

Which helps explain why the West remains the nation's fastest growing region. The 1990s and early 2000s saw the latest boom; the region's population grew at more than twice the national rate while job growth, business starts and income gains led the country. The promised land . . . still, all over again.

But at what cost? The West's latest growth surge has caused a new reckoning, not only among westerners but others who regard the West as the nation's harbinger. To many who live in or visit the region, the West's signature landscapes and sense of place appear to be receding behind a rising current of development and its predictable effects – a rapidly urbanizing landscape where traffic, sprawling subdivisions and gentrification are becoming commonplace. According to the American Farmland Trust, 250 acres of Colorado farmland are lost each day to development of one kind or another. Across the 11 western states, the National Resources Inventory reports that the percent of "built-up" non-federal land increased by half over the past 15 years. In all, experts believe that roughly one-third of the West's private land has been developed for residential, industrial or commercial uses, with no end in sight.

Enter Bill Travis, a western migrant by way of Florida and Massachusetts, who, from his post at the University of Colorado's Center for the American West, has made a career out of analyzing the region's seductiveness, not in literary terms but in the argot of land use planning and social geography. On meeting Bill Travis, you can't help but feel his passion for the West, as well as his concern. In Travis's eyes, the West is both a singular physical place and a place of mind, a majestic landscape and a precious idea. But today, in the waking hours of the new century, Travis believes the real West and the West of the imagination have arrived at a crossroads, with land use and development trends putting the region on a path at odds with its enduring values of wide open spaces, ruggedness and egalitarianism.

As Travis chronicles in *New Geographies*, the West's sprawling cities and resort areas are transforming the region's

141

iconic landscapes, fueled by population growth and an expanding economy. "[H]ow much resort growth, suburban sprawl, and rural land subdivision," Travis wonders, "can be accommodated while maintaining the West's remarkable natural wealth – its extensive wildlands and rich biodiversity – as well as its vibrant communities situated in an awe-inspiring landscape?"

Travis is an explorer; the tools of his trade are maps, charts, graphs, aerial photos – anything that will help him understand and interpret the landscape and patterns of human settlement. It is this on- and above-the-ground approach that gives Travis's account its accessibility and clarity. Which is his object. Travis isn't content with simply providing a rigorous study of the West's landscape changes; he seeks to inform people so they can begin to make better decisions about how, and where, the West will grow.

Building on the insights from his 1997 edited volume, *Atlas of the New West*, where Travis and his fellow authors described a "new" western economy and culture defined not by mining, logging and ranching but instead a post-industrial, services and amenities-based economy, Travis seeks to answer this seminal question by defining both the causes and effects of western land use patterns. With rich analysis and detail, he describes the different kinds of forces creating what he calls the West's four dominant "development geographies": Metro-Zones, Exurbs, Resort Zones and the Gentrifying Range. From Denver's sprawl to the ski slopes of Sun Valley to Montana's multi-million dollar ranches, Travis sees a dynamic, if unstable, patchwork of land use patterns made all the more complex by the region's nagging paradox: the very qualities that continue to attract people and businesses to the west in record numbers are withering under the pressure. The goose that laid the golden egg.

New Geographies is an academically veiled wake-up call.

Acknowledging the age-old failure of American planning institutions and practices to substantially influence western land use patterns, Travis holds up a mirror to the region and asks the (rhetorical) question, "If this is what things looks like, what do we want to do about it?" In his final two chapters, Travis prescribes a diverse set of measures to get the West back on track. From grassroots organizing and advocacy, to the use of sophisticated planning technology, to rules and regulation, Travis pulls from his holster not a six-gun loaded with silver bullets but instead an assortment of strategies and tools designed to help strike the proper balance – more like a creative tension   between preserving the West's natural and cultural assets and developing them in support of the region's people, places and economic possibilities.

The West's greatest truth is that it is a place constantly in the process of becoming, of migrating from where it is to where it wants to be – the "golden age" of Bishop Berkeley's poem, Stegner's "geography of hope." And perhaps there's no end to this migration, this journey, no Pacific coastline marking its terminus, no final act in its epic drama. And isn't that the point? *New Geographies* teaches us that the West's virtues, and its vices, stem from the same source: it's open-endedness, its awesome spaces stretching to infinitude, its embrace of new forms, ideas and lifestyles. What makes the West different, and will be its salvation, is its willingness to keep forging ahead in search of itself, and a new geography to match.

Part III : The Planet

September 11. Google Earth. WTO. India. China. MySpace. Kyoto. Iraq. Oil. Coal. Immigration. Mexico. Ice Caps. Outsourcing.

There are so many signs of a globalizing planet it's hard to keep track. Thomas Friedman describes a new "flat" world of commerce and culture. Anthony Appiah points to "Cosmopolitanism" as the emergent, or more precisely resurgent, way of the world, the continuous mixing or "contaminating" of people and societies over time, never achieving a state of "purity," always in flux. It's this horizontalness and blending that make the idea of a new global consciousness and commons imaginable. But if there is a primary catalyst for this new world order climate change has to be a leading candidate.

Like all environmental issues, climate change, as a scientific phenomenon and social fact, defies borders. Due to its very scope, it causes individuals, no matter how parochial or atomistic in their mindset, to think bigger, outside their usual context and spatial and temporal scales. Paradoxically, the challenge of climate change contains the seeds of a solution. If individuals, companies and nations are at fault for endangering the global climate as a result of emitting tons of greenhouse gases in pursuit of their self-interest – the uber-tragedy of the commons – then, at least in theory, only acting collectively, as a team, can we combat the threat. Another case of necessity begetting invention.

But how do individuals become motivated to act on global problems whose effects might not be immediately or directly felt? How does the micro I become the macro We? Part III addresses the threat of human-induced climate change and some of the actions that can be taken to combat it. It suggests that our greatest planetary problem might not be climate change after all but the challenge of collective action it presents, a potential road-block between our best intentions and achieving social change at a scale and pace equal to the threat.

The writings in this chapter reflect on the nature of capitalism and its consequences – for people, place and the planet. It is cliche to criticize capitalism's many foibles, and indeed there is much to criticize. But if nothing else, capitalism of the type operating in the U.S. has proved a very hardy, resilient system. It's not going away any time soon. And who says we can't create a version of capitalism that's a bridge, and not a barrier, to a global, sustainable future?

Part III also examines environmentalism – as a movement, worldview and framework for economic development. Like capitalism, it's not hard to point out environmentalism's shortcomings. Attacked as elitist, racist and downright hypocritical, environmentalists have taken their fair share of body blows over the years, and not without justification in some cases. But it seems environmentalism is finally beginning to realize its promise as a true social movement, beginning to turn the corner toward an expansive, inspiring and democratic social vision any right-minded person would be hard-pressed to resist. Green, some would say, has become the new Red, White and Blue. Combine all those colors together and maybe, just maybe, we're on to something.

Land Use and Development as Toxic as Any Other Threat

The Boston Globe
April 2000

Earth Day 2000 will be celebrated around the country this week. Under the banner "New Energy for a New Era," the organizers have offered up a clarion call to end our reliance on dirty 19th-century energy sources like oil and coal and shift to clean, renewable technologies such as wind and solar power. The campaign hopes to enlist half a billion people worldwide by Saturday and, given past success, that goal is well within reach.

Yet, as important as energy is as a cause of environmental harms such as global climate change, air pollution, and oil spills, by focusing all of our attention on a single issue, environmentalists are relegating to second-class status an equally significant, though less media-friendly, problem: Land use and development, both in the United States and abroad, which have fundamentally altered the planet in a way no other force has. Population growth, migration, low-density settlement, and unplanned development have contributed mightily to global and local environmental threats while consuming land and habitat at ever-increasing rates.

Roughly a third of greenhouse gases comes from cars, trucks, buses, and planes traveling the great distances created by sprawling development patterns. In the United States, most water pollution is the result of runoff from overdeveloped cities and suburbs, where cars and residential subdivisions have unleashed a host of uncontrolled pollutants into rivers, streams, and ground water.

Since 1970, the land area of metropolitan Los Angeles has

grown by 300 percent, outpacing population growth by a factor of 7. (It's no wonder mountain lions have become more frequent visitors to Los Angeles neighborhoods.) Meanwhile, metropolitan Chicago saw its land area expand by 46 percent while its population grew by a paltry 4 percent. The same story holds for most big American cities.

Land use and development decisions are precursors to the environmental damage caused by energy production and consumption. Before oil or coal are extracted, or power plants are built, decisions are made allowing or forbidding such activities. Likewise, before auto manufacturing facilities or highways are constructed, or before housing subdivisions are developed, land use decisions come into play.

Yet land use and development issues are not dealt with by our system of environmental laws, and the Environmental Protection Agency and most federal and state environmental agencies have almost no jurisdiction over them; instead, such issues are left to local zoning boards and planning commissions.

It is this localized authority that provides ordinary citizens a chance to participate in decisions affecting their immediate environment. Although often influenced by powerful, monied interests, almost all land use decisions require a bare minimum of public involvement, especially from those who live or work next to a proposed project, be it a housing subdivision or highway.

Fortunately, communities across the country are beginning to seize control over land use and development decisions, heralding a new era of environmental activism and democratic renewal, as well as community improvement.

For example, in Boston's Roxbury neighborhood, decades of white flight and disinvestment have left not only high unemployment and poverty rates but also countless abandoned, contaminated lots – brownfields – among other environmental hazards. The Dudley Street Neighborhood Initiative (DSNI) has engaged citizens and other key stakeholders in a multiyear planning effort to convert these environmental liabilities into community assets and a material base for food production, called the Urban Agriculture Strategy.

With a pilot bioshelter/greenhouse soon to be built on a local brownfield, DSNI is cleaning up the contaminated land, reclaiming Roxbury's agrarian past, providing jobs, and restoring a sense of place to an area that for so long has been a symbol of decay and danger. The initiative is creating an urban village and, in the process, going against the grain of agribusiness and a food industry that relies heavily on toxic pesticides and dangerous labor conditions.

Meanwhile, just down the road in the South Bay, DSNI is working with other groups to promote green development on the site of the former city incinerator, abandoned for over 25 years.

A few thousand miles to the west, the success of the Steamboat Springs ski resort, and the flight of many urban residents from congested, sprawling Rocky Mountain cities like Denver and Salt Lake have brought unprecedented development to rugged Routt County, Colorado. Developers will pay up to 20 times the farm value of land, and as a result, the Yampa and Elk River Valleys are being chopped up into 35-acre lot subdivisions, notoriously exempted from land use controls by state law.

Fearing the loss of their rural economy and culture, ranchers, environmentalists, local officials, and professional planners have together created a county open-space plan, relying on public investment and private measures like conservation easements to save the land. (They've even written a handbook on how to live in a rural county, with advice such as: Don't take offense at the smell of cattle manure.)

What's more, the Nature Conservancy has changed its traditional strategy of simply buying up islands of land and prohibiting human uses. Instead, it has teamed up with ranchers, their traditional nemesis, to promote working landscapes and ranching, while educating ranchers on ecosystem protection. They are even helping develop for-profit ventures to help ranchers stay in business; ranchers now sell organic beef raised on protected lands, and blankets from local sheep.

What these stories reflect is a pivotal realignment of environmentalism away from exclusively legal or regulatory approaches, based on individual pollutants and single media and handed down from on-high, to a more integrated, bottom-up approach. This new "civic environmentalism" is aimed at overall community and ecosystem health, including social and economic health.

It is more planning-based and preventive than traditional strategies, which have tended to focus on the biggest, most readily controllable pollution sources, blending legal measures with fiscal policy, sound science, new forms of governance and civic will. And, unlike traditional environmentalism, civic environmentalism actually promotes development – the kind that is good for the environment and the community.

Most important, it promotes civic engagement and a public vision, and as it does, transcends geography, income, and race – demonstrating that our environment and community respond to each other, are one in a dialectical sense.

"To build a better motor," the noted conservationist Aldo Leopold wrote, "we tap the uttermost powers of the human brain; to build a better countryside, we throw dice."

On Earth Day 2000, there is no question we possess the know-how to build better technologies using clean, renewable energy sources. Now we must create the political will to act on that ability. This year's campaign, we hope, will do so.

But this Earth Day should also mark the beginning of another new effort by citizens, community groups, and environmentalists to exercise their power to affect everyday land use and development decisions. Those are the decisions that, in the long run, will determine our environmental and social progress.

Capitalism and the Environment

Metamute Magazine
August 2001

> *William Shutkin, author of* The Land That Could Be:
> Environmentalism and Democracy in the Twenty-First
> Century, *gives five reasons for believing that democratic
> capitalism and vital eco-systems could happily co-exist.*

1. Capitalism is a Construct.

To believe that capitalism is inherently limited vis-à-vis
environmental goals is to give up the battle before it's been
joined. Like all man-made systems, capitalism is constantly
being shaped, revised, and reinvented by those communities
who adopt and use it. As with any human institution, it is
subject to abuse and malfeasance, but has proved increasingly
open to progressive reform through shareholder activism,
corporate social responsibility techniques, social policies, and
other interventions.

2. Capitalism is Only Part of the Equation.

As an economic model, capitalism is just that. It does not
and cannot purport to be a comprehensive system of social
governance or social values. Capitalism on its own can be an
awful environmental menace (not to mention its sometimes
evil social effects). But economic activities are conducted
within a larger system of social relationships, and rely on legal
and political systems to temper and manage their effects. In a
representative democracy and liberal legal order such as exists
in the U.S., this means there is the potential to deal with
capitalism's negative environmental externalities i.e., pollution
and waste, through social policy, regulation and adjudication.
That firms and markets have yet to be effectively regulated or

held accountable for their environmentally harmful actions suggests that the political and legal orders have not functioned as effectively as they should.

3. The Paradox and Promise of American Environmentalism.

No other nation on the planet can claim an environmental traditional as strong and enduring as the American environmental movement. No doubt this is in part a function of the fact that as early as the beginning of the 19th century, concerned citizens started to worry about the pace and scale of environmental destruction brought about by mercantilist enterprises bent on exploiting natural resources as part of a simultaneous nation-building and commercial effort. Capitalists, and Americans in general, have historically resisted efforts aimed at putting the public interest ahead of private gain. But as Americans have become more educated about and engaged in environmental efforts, the demand for more "social democracy" and social responsibility has grown, suggesting the strong possibility of a greener capitalist culture over time.

4. No Other System's Proved More Environmentally Responsible.

Unfortunately, no other social order has proved more environmentally responsible than America's capitalist/liberal democratic system. Every large, industrialized nation has experienced or is in the process of experiencing large-scale environmental degradation owing to the depletion of common resources and the attendant negative environmental externalities. Because of the sheer size of the American economy and a uniquely aggressive consumer culture, the nation's ecological footprint is larger than any other. But we must not assume it has to be this way; the reformist tradition within the capitalist/liberal democratic system is robust and can help create new environmentally friendly ways of reforming economic development.

5. Natural Capitalism and Sustainable Development.

Emerging theories and practices of economic development are finally coming to recognize the immeasurable value of nature's goods and services and the malleability of capitalist constructs. Ideas like "natural capitalism" and "sustainable development" suggest there are feasible methods for protecting natural resources while supporting viable economic activity. From green design and industrial ecology to green tax policy and sustainable land use planning, new policies and techniques are being developed to "green" the way firms and market behave, and the way communities and regions physically grow and change over time.

Green Development Connects Nature and Neighborhoods

The Boston Business Journal
February 2002

Even the gray January sky couldn't dull the unveiling of Boston's greenest building, introduced in mid-January at a groundbreaking on part of the former Boston State Hospital site in Mattapan. Set to open in the Spring, 2002, the new George Robert White Environmental Conservation Center will be home to the Massachusetts Audubon Society's new nature center and signals a bold new direction not only for development but, equally important, for environmentalism.

The nature center is significant because it is one of the few, and easily the most ambitious, local examples of environmentally responsible development, demonstrating that such "green" facilities can not only be built but at a competitive price compared to more conventional buildings. Aside from its high-tech features like a geothermal climate-control system, electricity-generating shingles, and roof-top solar panels, reducing the building's energy use by 30 percent, the nature center will restore a long-languishing habitat for wild turkey, pheasant, and hawks and provide more than two miles of natural trails in the heart of the city. What's more, the planning for the project engaged a racially and economically diverse group of local residents and organizations, incorporating their vision for a greener, cleaner community while building neighborhood support.

In addition, the nature center gives a boost to green development advocates who are constantly on the look out for demonstration projects to point to when responding to the nay-sayers who claim that environmentally responsible development is too expensive. The project adds to a small but growing portfolio of green projects in and around Boston that are creating a new, better standard for urban planning, design and construction.

Just as important as the nature center's impact on development practices is what the project says about environmentalism in the twenty-first century. It is no small irony that the first project to break ground on the 100-acre state hospital site, where for more than a decade city and state planners have been trying unsuccessfully to bring new, mixed use development, is being spearheaded by one of the nation's oldest environmental groups. After all, environmental organizations like the Audubon Society have traditionally fought tooth-and-nail against development, not supported it. Nor have they usually been associated with the urban environment, known more for their work protecting endangered birds and other wildlife in more rural, more remote settings.

Meanwhile, lower-income communities of color like Mattapan and nearby Roxbury, frustrated by persistent pollution and blighted land, have also waged war against unwelcome developers but most often without the assistance of environmental groups like the Audubon Society, whose membership has never been well represented in minority communities.

The nature center suggests that environmentalism is evolving from an elitist movement fixated on preserving undeveloped land and resources to a more democratic, more proactive program aimed at building healthy, sustainable communities across geographic, economic and cultural lines. More than just a physical structure, the nature center is an emblem for an expanding environmental constituency, reaching deep into the lost landscapes of urban neighborhoods, that is doing more than simply opposing development. They're actually doing it, in ways at once economically viable and environmentally responsible and in places long overdue.

The city of Boston and the Massachusetts Audubon Society should be applauded for this innovative project and the environmental vision it embodies. But the true success of the nature center will come not from its energy savings or even the number of visitors but its impact on future development in the region. And who knows, maybe other environmental groups will be inspired to break out their hammers and start building. Let's hope so.

Howls Over Cape Wind Farm Drown Out Merits

The Boston Business Journal
October 2002

The gathering storm over the proposal by Cape Wind to build 170 425-foot wind turbines six miles off Cape Cod has ramifications equal to some of the biggest environmental controversies of the last three decades, rivaling the endangered spotted owl, the Exxon Valdez oil spill, the hole in the ozone layer, and Love Canal.

The reason is simple: Unless communities in Massachusetts and others across the country are able to implement large-scale renewable energy and other "green" projects like the Cape Wind proposal, we are bound to repeat the environmental mistakes of the past.

The merits of the proposal speak for themselves. With minimal environmental impacts (and all development, no matter how green, has environmental effects), the wind project would on average provide enough energy for at least half the Cape and Islands. When the wind is right, the project would supply all their energy needs.

Local source, local production, local use, all at an affordable price, in perpetuity: That's the definition of sustainability. In an imperfect world, environmental goods don't get much better than that.

So what's all the fuss about? Like all "not in my back yard" campaigns, the project opponents, the Alliance to Protect Nantucket Sound, claim a host of wrongs to the marine ecosystem and their property. The wind farm will industrialize Nantucket Sound, they claim, and in the process impair the fishery and their view.

But what makes this case categorically different, and so important, is that whereas classic NIMBY campaigns involve projects whose local environmental impacts outweigh their local environmental or economic upsides, this one is just the opposite.

Consider the case of regional trash incinerators, like the one in Haverhill. It accepts 1,650 tons of solid waste every day from dozens of outlying communities far removed from the facility's impacts. Overshadowing the local benefits from jobs and tax revenue are the incinerator's undeniable costs: drastically diminished property values for nearby residents coupled with significant environmental harm from pollutants like mercury and dioxin.

The Cape Wind proposal presents a stark contrast. In exchange for putting up with the barely visible facility several miles off shore, the Cape and Islands alone receive all the direct benefits: clean, affordable energy.

The secondary benefits are just as compelling: Renewable-energy projects like Cape Wind are the first and most critical step in breaking the downward spiral of U.S. dependence on fossil fuels and the myriad hazards stemming from it – from war in Arabian oil fields, to broken tankers in Prince William Sound, to rising sea levels due to climate change – of particular concern to the Cape and Islands.

Moreover, with a growing interest in green technology here and abroad, the Cape wind farm is the region's most significant ecotourism opportunity, on par with similar projects in Palm Springs, California, Denmark and Australia.

The story of the Cape Wind proposal is not about wind turbines, or fisheries, or pristine seascapes. It is about the capacity of environmentalists – of citizens – to match their public positions with the private choices necessary to move toward a more environmentally and economically sustainable way of life. It's about the ability of environmentalists to put their money where their mouth is by dispelling the myth that industrial development is inherently bad.

Regrettably, the Cape Wind opposition plays right into the worst stereotype of environmentalists as wealthy elites who are all for environmental protection, except when it affects their back yard. That's the reason you won't find an incinerator in Weston or a trash-transfer station on Beacon Hill.

The only social justice issue bound up in this controversy are the tens of thousands of men and women, most of them poor and people of color, who end up going to war in places like Kuwait to defend our nation's deadly addiction to fossil fuels, all because we at home are unwilling to make the right choices, public and private, to achieve energy independence.

The controversy also points to a misguided romanticism that has characterized the environmental movement for two centuries. For too long, environmentalists have held out the notion that the environments most worth saving are pristine, remote places, sparsely settled if at all, and devoid of industry or urbanization. This has resulted in a false choice between, on the one hand, pristine places, and on the other, dirty, industrialized areas.

Nature is more complicated than that. Most of our landscapes have at one time or another been worked, developed or industrialized. Those that haven't we call parks and wilderness.

If we are going to live responsibly in our places, whether in cities or rural communities, we must learn to create new landscapes somewhere between the pristine and the fallen. This means that some of our cherished natural areas – mountaintops, meadows, even Nantucket Sound – will need to change to accommodate the uses and technologies necessary to sustain our very civilization. The result can still be beauty, but of a different, more human, kind.

It is in the nature of renewable energy that we think and

act locally; we can't change the direction of the prevailing winds or move the sun, at least not now. But by embracing projects like Cape Wind, environmentalists can help point the way to new worlds and new opportunities based on a clear commitment to the public good and a green vision of development.

Failing this, environmentalists risk simply whistling in the wind, as silent as a high-tech turbine, while pollution and waste continue to claim our communities and the planet.

Paper Promises

Grist Magazine
May 2003

These are tough times for environmentalists. What with the Bush Administration's frontal assault on environmental policy, drastic funding cuts and layoffs in state environmental programs, and a looming war with Iraq over what many consider to be our undying addiction to oil. It's thus fitting, if not a bit disheartening, that along come two books whose central message is that it's not easy being green, no matter what the circumstances. Allen Hershkowitz's *Bronx Ecology: Blueprint for a New Environmentalism* and Lis Harris's *Tilting at Mills: Green Dreams, Dirty Dealings, and the Corporate Squeeze* are companion accounts of what happens when an environmentalist, armed with missionary zeal and more than a dash of ego, meets the gritty reality of politics and planning in the environmentally unfit South Bronx. The protagonist in question is Allen Hershkowitz who, as a senior scientist with the Natural Resources Defense Council (NRDC), spent the 1980s advocating for tougher laws to deal with the country's mounting solid waste problems.

Then one day in 1992, a new solution dawned on him. He would build the Bronx Community Paper Company, a state-of-the-art paper recycling mill on an abandoned, polluted rail yard in the rough and tumble Mott Haven/Port Morris section. The facility would not only would provide 600 permanent jobs to an area with unemployment rates as high as 75 percent, but it would be a model of "green" development, transforming a 30-acre brownfield site into a low-emission, energy- and water-efficient recycling plant that would help deal with the 10,000 tons of waste paper produced every day by residents and businesses in New York City.

To sell his vision, Hershkowitz needed a community partner to provide credibility and help grease the skids for his big plan. The Banana Kelly Community Improvement Association, a non-profit developer in the South Bronx, fit the bill and quickly embraced a partnership with Hershkowitz. With Banana Kelly on board, NRDC moved forward aggressively with the project, retaining Maya Lin, the famed architect of the National Vietnam Memorial in Washington, DC, to design the facility and enlisting President Bill Clinton, who praised the project in his 1996 book, Between Hope and History.

But if the story sounds too good to be true, that's because it was. The South Bronx Clean Air Coalition, an ad hoc community group, challenged the paper plant proposal, claiming pollution from the facility would exacerbate the area's already poor air quality, another violation in a long line of environmental injustices. They had other plans for the site, including reviving the long-defunct rail yard as a bustling inter-modal transportation center.

After several years of litigation, a New York appeals court ruled in 1997 that NRDC and Banana Kelly could proceed with the project. The legal victory, however, was short-lived. Mounting costs, fraying relationships between Banana Kelly, NRDC, and their backers, and other problems eventually sunk the project in 2000. NRDC vowed never again to try to play the role of developer. Banana Kelly, meanwhile, became the subject of intense media scrutiny as the shady financial dealings of its high-profile director, Yolanda Rivera, and her deputies came to light. Hershkowitz's lofty vision lay in shambles, another casualty of the cruel city's toxic environment.

Hershkowitz, ever the technocrat, is a better analyzer than storyteller, and, in keeping with this, his account reads more like a sustainable development handbook than a human-interest story. He does a good job spelling out the technical and public policy issues underlying the mill proposal, such as industrial ecology. IE is a new model for development that, as its name implies, joins environmental and economic goals by advancing a set of design and production methods that mimic the reuse and replenishing functions of natural systems, resulting in the prevention, and not merely the control, of pollution and waste. Concepts like IE are a mouthful, and Hershkowitz does the reader a service by explicating them in a way that is at once rigorous and easily understood. He also brings a genuine enthusiasm to the more technical subject matter, adding to the book's readability.

Harris, a Columbia writing professor and former New Yorker contributor, is a good storyteller, but to a fault. She's too fawning in her appraisal of Hershkowitz and his NRDC colleagues (save for one, an African-American staffer who Harris takes to task for her conflicting allegiances to NRDC, on the one hand, and the community groups, on the other), whom Harris considers white knights. She lays the blame for the project's collapse entirely at the doorstep of the community groups, as well as the project's financiers, portrayed as preternaturally inept and rapaciously greedy, respectively. But Harris is too facile in her analysis of community politics and the challenge of urban redevelopment, which are not reducible to a simple morality tale. There are too many variables in play, from complex financial arrangements and history-laden strife between stakeholder groups, to arcane regulations and uncertain environmental risks.

Where Hershkowitz's and Harris's accounts both fall short is in helping the reader understand the larger meaning of the South Bronx tale, which is nothing less than the story of American environmentalism at the beginning of the twenty-first century. Despite the movement's proud tradition and many successes, U.S. environmentalism needs a new vision, especially given today's political climate. As the paper mill story suggests, environmentalists have learned they must expand their focus beyond their core, upper-middle class white constituency and a concern for parks and wilderness to people of color, the poor, and the inner-city. At the same time, environmentalists are beginning to realize they must do more than just stop unwanted development, or point out when someone else is doing something wrong. Like NRDC's South Bronx effort, they should actively pursue plans for economic development that deliver not only jobs and dollars but environmental benefits as well.

No small feat. As the paper mill saga shows, trying to bring together communities and cultures, environmental restoration and jobs, around a good idea is tough work. Environmentalists, for their part, simply aren't well adapted to working with diverse constituencies, much less playing the part of industrial developer. The result can be a lot of missteps, miscommunication, and distrust of the kind that befell Hershkowitz and his partners. Most community residents, meanwhile, are too quick to resort to Not In My Back Yard tactics when confronted with new development proposals. This "collective action" problem means that even the best of proposals can fall prey to misguided claims or dissembling.

Undertaking a project as ambitious as the South Bronx paper mill might well have been quixotic, as the title of Harris's book suggests. But transforming two centuries' worth of industrial development, and the environmental movement bent on thwarting it, won't happen overnight. Like natural systems, the process will be slow, incremental, non-linear – a series of failures and mistakes over time. Such is the nature of evolution, and social change. It starts with a vision and gets harder from there. But it can be done. It must be done. The future of the South Bronx, if not the planet, depends on it.

Wine and Woods

Northern Woodlands Magazine
Summer 2004

I like wine – a lush Napa Valley cabernet, a big Barolo, a white burgundy from Montrachet. It's the earthiness, the taste as old as water. Which is why I happened to notice the fleet of Vermont varietals filling the shelves last summer, from the homeliest general store to the fanciest wine merchant in Burlington. Turns out winemaking in cooler regions like Vermont has gotten easier in recent years as temperatures around the globe have increased, about one degree on average since 1900 and more in the higher latitudes. Warm air causes sugar inside grapes to be released which in turn leads to ripeness, and wine.

In Vermont, the moderating effect on the area's climate of Lake Champlain, around which most of the state's vineyards can be found, has clearly helped local winemakers. But the recent rise in the number and quality of wines produced, and the stories from other winemaking regions like Oregon and Italy, which have seen dramatic improvements in their wines on account of sharply warmer temperatures, suggest that global climate change is also a factor.

Now as much as I like wine, I like trees better. I'm a woodlands guy, not a vineyarder. So I have to ask myself, if the region's winemakers are benefiting from higher temperatures, what does this mean for our forests? After all, what climate change may give, it can also take away. In my view, the most significant change to New England's woodlands in the last decade is the realization that climate change might fundamentally alter their make-up and use. Take the maple sugar industry, for example. The delicate chemistry that regulates maple sap flows will likely be disrupted by warmer winter days and nights, reducing the amount and quality of sap produced. In addition, sugar maples and other tree species in the North Woods, especially the broadleaf trees, stand to be harmed by rising temperatures as severe ice storms, like the one in 1998, become more common, wreaking havoc on the forest canopy. This, in turn, will affect not only the wood products industry but the very look and feel of the forest.

I don't know about you, but I like my North Woods just the way they are, remembering that it's the region's colder climate, among other key factors, that best distinguishes these forest ecosystems from their more temperate cousins to the south. I fear the effects climate change may bring, however uncertain they may be, and can only hope that as forest users we do all we can to keep what makes the North Woods the North Woods.

Knotweed

Vermont Public Radio
June 2005

There's a plague among us. It goes by the name Japanese Knotweed. I thought I had left this insidious herb behind when my family and I moved from the city to Vermont last year. Boy, was I mistaken.

Known euphemistically as New England Bamboo, knotweed is a roadside plant that, like so many invasive species, was introduced from Europe via the Far East. With its alternate leaves and arching stalks, it looks at first glance like the gentle Hobblebush, an understory shrub of Vermont's mountain forest. Anything but gentle, knotweed is spreading across the state at a rapid clip, from downtown lots to remote wilderness paths.

After we installed a new septic system at our house last year, I was horrified to find that within days, small red stems with oblong leaves began to sprout. The gravel used to backfill the leach field must have carried with it Knotweed. I immediately began pulling out the young plants and burning them.

Unfortunately, thanks to its thick underground stem and endless supply of carbohydrates, every single fiber and cell of the plant has to be stripped out of the earth, or it will regenerate. No small labor considering its root stem can grow quickly to tens of feet.

That knotweed is outcompeting native plants is bad enough. But what's really troublesome is its effect on my sense of place. I remember hiking down one a section of the Catamount trail in Weston many summers ago. About two miles from the nearest road, I came across a large stand of knotweed stretching about 40 feet along the trail. In an instant, I was no longer in the Green Mountain National Forest. Instead, I felt as if I could have been in any urbanized setting, any city where invasive species like knotweed are so common thanks to their high tolerance for blight. It was disorienting.

Observing the spread of invasives like knotweed, the writer David Quammen warns that we're heading toward a "planet of weeds," a place where crows, kudzu and cockroaches dominate, where super-species whose ability to thrive in the most extreme environments has given them a competitive edge in a world where the line between the pristine and developed is no longer so clear

Maybe it's the case that I'm too much of a purist in believing that certain plants simply don't belong in certain places, that the spread of Knotweed is an unqualified threat. After all, we live on a dynamic planet; change, not equilibrium, is the norm. But what is place if it isn't something defined by those things that are unique to it? And what's the fate of Vermont's distinctive understory plants in the face of Knotweed's homogenizing effect?

This summer, I asked my kids to join me in a Knotweed Patrol, to stand guard against the invader along our roadside and fields. I might not be able to save the planet from Knotweed, but I can sure as heck do something about my own backyard.

The Future Is Now:
Planning As If Tomorrow Mattered

Vermont Planners Association/Vermont Department of
Housing and Community Affairs Planning Celebration
Keynote Address
October 2005

Many thanks to Sue Minter, John Hall, Deb Sachs
and your colleagues at the Department of Housing and
Community Affairs and the Vermont Planners Association for
having me here this morning. What a great celebration. I'm
honored to be a part of it.

Today, in the spirit of this event and the theme of
Planning and Implementation, I want to talk to you about
the importance of planning and the idea that planning
cannot, must not, be seen as separate from action, from
implementation. I want to talk about planning as an essential
act of democratic citizenship, of community, and about the
ways in which planners and their many different kinds of
partners are finally beginning to act as if tomorrow matters, as
if what we do today will shape the course and quality of life
for years, generations, to come.

And let me start by relating to you a recent conversation
I had with my wife, Sally. We were talking a few weeks ago
about parenthood. I've got two kids, a son, 4, and a daughter,
7. We were having that somewhat uncomfortable, disquieting
discussion spouses have about as infrequently as they can
about how we were doing as parents, how we've performed
in our job to date, individually and as a team. It's a hard
conversation, at least for me, especially when, like me, you've
got kids who swear too much, who can't get to school on time
and who otherwise often make you feel like parenting is your
weakest skill set.

But as we finished up our talk, I said to Sally that, ultimately, I would judge my parenting performance not so much by the day-to-day, the little episodes and outbursts, but by the long term. I would judge my performance, in other words, by what my children, Olivia and Shepard, become, by what they make of their lives going forward – the interests and attitudes they cultivate, the relationships they forge, the experiences they have and, finally and perhaps most importantly, their contributions to building a better world.

OK, so maybe because I'm a planner, or at least hang out with planners (I'm actually a lawyer who only taught planners and now works with them), my perspective on parenting is a bit skewed. But I think the analogy really holds. Planning, like parenthood, is about doing things today that will help create the conditions for a better tomorrow. As parenting is to the family, planning is to the community: a fundamental responsibility, that can be undertaken with skill or poorly, but one that must be performed.

Like democracy, planning is not something we have, it's something we do. Planning is doing, is implementing. It derives its meaning from its application. In other words, there is no planning apart from implementation. Planning in the absence of action we call words, documents. It's like the poet William Carlos Williams said about images: "No ideas but in things." Show me, prove it, do it.

And never has the need to do planning, to move from ideas to things, to action, been as great as it is right now, today.

Just look around. In the last decade alone, a constellation of diverse but connected circumstances have conspired to shift our basic understandings and expectations of the world around us and how we navigate it. These include transformations in technology, cataclysmic geo-political events, unprecedented surges in real estate markets and, most recently, a flood of Biblical proportions, each of which have literally shaken our nation, if not the world, to a new understanding of both the promise and the peril of this new century.

Just as the internet has emboldened us to connect to and experience the world in exciting new ways, so have a host of threats emerged to make us tentative and afraid: the threat of terrorism in the post-9/11 order; the fear of natural disasters after Hurricane Katrina; and a less dramatic but equally unnerving condition, the affordable housing crisis that's eating at the very fabric of the American dream for so many of our fellow citizens.

Surely, the ante has been upped.

So much so that none other than Paul Volker, you remember him, the stoggy, cigar-smoking former Fed Reserve Board Chair and no shrinking violet, recently declared in a stark and somewhat cynical mood: "America is over." "Circumstances," he said, "seem to me as dangerous and intractable as any I can remember. . . . What really concerns me is that there seems to be so little willingness or capacity to do anything about it."

And isn't that why we're here, why you're here. I submit to you, my fellow planners, that distress, the feeling that things are out of control, is an ideology, not a fact, and that planning – planning as vision, planning as action – is the perfect response, indeed the only response, to Volker's despair and to the pervasive anxiety that seems to have gripped the nation.

And what do I mean by Planning Vision and Planning Action? Planning vision is about the ends – the world we want, or could have. It's the idea that to do things differently, we have to first perceive them differently. It's the art and science of seeing across issues areas and problems, from local to global, from private to public, from health to environment, from housing to jobs, from individual to community, to a greater sum than these parts. It's making connections between seemingly unrelated data, events and circumstances. It's engaging diverse viewpoints and interests so as to build the buy-in and support that any democratic enterprise requires. Planning vision is alchemy and prophecy.

Planning action is the execution of that vision, it's the means, the implementation half that completes the whole. It's the care and precision with which a team designs and executes a set of measures – whether policy, institutional, market or cultural – to get us where we want or need to go. It's engineering a program of activity that will create positive change revealed in the built, the natural, the economic and social systems in which our lives occur.

The two work hand in hand, the vision and the action. They comprise any true planning effort. But this is theory, the intellectual response to Volcker's ideology of despair. What about the practice?

Let me give you a few examples of planning on-the-ground that I believe offer signs of hope amidst the uncertainty and distress and that justify the kind of celebration today's event is all about.

Vermont's a good place to start. Like many of you, I'm a huge fan of the Vermont Housing and Conservation Board. The Board was the brainchild of land trusts, affordable housing advocates and historic preservation groups who came together in 1986 to form the Housing and Conservation Coalition, a smart growth organization, a planning organization, before the term was even invented. They had a planning vision: to help conserve working farms and other natural and historic resources while supporting affordable housing and community development. Preserve the best of the past, promote the needs of the future.

In 1987, that vision became the law establishing the Board. Eighteen years later the Board has helped conserve over 325,000 acres of Vermont's countryside while underwriting the construction of roughly 7500 units of perpetually affordable housing.

The recently completed City Edge project in South Burlington, for example, a partnership between the Board and the Burlington Community Land Trust, was featured in the *New York Times* last month, its 60 units making a real dent in the affordable housing crisis facing Chittenden County. The Board has been a key player in not just preserving Vermont's landscapes but creating places, real places, in the fullest sense, where nature and culture, past and present, wealthy and low-income are linked together by that one great denominator, the land.

Or how about Hayden, Colorado where, in this small town of 1500 on the outskirts of Steamboat Springs in the northwestern part of the state, 150 residents – 10 percent of the town – showed up to a planning meeting last November to decide their town's fate: Would they become a bedroom community of gated, large lot subdivisions or would they build on their existing assets, their historic downtown and ranching communities?

The people of Hayden, under the leadership of the town's planning director, Russ Martin, determined that they needed to take action. They resolved to amend their comprehensive plan and zoning regs to better reflect their vision and respond to the changes looming at their doorstep, in this case a proposal to build a 2000-unit gated golf community on 930 acres outside the town center.

This small town used state-of-the-art technology and old-fashioned meeting techniques to chart their course for the future. At the November capstone meeting, participants used CommunityViz, the Orton Family Foundation's 3D visualization tool, as well as keypad polling, a wireless PDA device that allows participants to register their votes anonymously and qualitatively in real time, in deciding that the town simply couldn't afford to support large residential development in the absence of a commercial development strategy for downtown. What's more, they decided that a revitalized downtown, an improved school system and affordable housing for workers and ranchers was their key to sustainability. They amended their plan and rules accordingly.

Or look at Chula Vista, California, where the county, the state and a collection of non-profit organizations is developing a plan for the country's first "energy efficient community development" on a former 1500 acre ranchland site proposed for mixed use development. In light of southern California's growing population, sprawling development patterns and persistent air and water pollution problems, this innovative planning project seeks to establish a new baseline for mixed-use development in California and the country as a whole. It will model the energy needs of the proposed subdivision and its impacts on energy consumption and air emissions for residential, commercial, industrial and institutional structures and for water, wastewater and solid waste management processes.

The project will also model transportation infrastructure, patterns and strategies for energy consumption and emission impacts using both quantitative factors such as housing density and road patterns, and qualitative factors such as the probability that residents will actually choose alternative modes of transportation.

Essentially, the Chula Vista project is doing for community development what the U.S. Green Building Council did for commercial development: establishing a benchmark of environmental, social and economic excellence that governments and the private market will respond to. In a sense, each of these planning innovations, where vision and action have come together, represents a corrective response to the past. These are really experiments in social learning, where a group of people, called planners, who have identified certain negative patterns of land use and development have said, "let's change this pattern, let's create a new legacy, a new model."

And look at all the new models. Old development patterns are falling away; they no longer make sense. Urban areas are trying to become more rural, trying to restore their greenspace, gardens and waterfronts. Rural areas are looking to densify, to cluster housing and mixed use in their village centers like cities, and are inviting new immigrant communities who are changing the cultures of these places. Meanwhile, suburbs are changing to, embracing density and urban forms, protecting working landscapes and welcoming diverse populations like their rural counterparts. Spatial patterns, and more importantly, communities, are changing. We have the opportunity to create the new patterns, the new blueprints. Distress, helplessness is an ideology, not a fact. And isn't this the gift of planning, isn't this why we celebrate this practice, this profession? Think about it: Planning is one of the great human attributes distinguishing us from the rest of the animal order. Planning is what evolved when we no longer had to worry about that next predator around the bend, about living hand to mouth, day to day. Planning is what happens when you're fortunate enough to be able to contemplate a better future. It is a gift of will, of intention, of the generative spirit to create the change we seek in the world rather than being ruled by it.

"I plan, therefore I am," should be the new Cartesian credo, and celebrations of this kind should be more common. Planners, at their best, are prophesiers, exercising that most special and singular of human capabilities, imagination. It is planners who, in the words of Carlos Williams again, first hear the "rumors of a separate world."

As you spend the day talking about all manner of planning

issues – from public participation to housing to zoning
– don't lose sight of what it is you're actually talking about:
remaking the world. Planning is a gift. It deserves to be
celebrated.

Many thanks for listening. I look forward to meeting and
working with many of you in the years to come. Enjoy the
celebration.

India

Perspectives on Place Blog
December 2005

India is nothing less than an urbanizing, industrializing juggernaut, smarter than China, as high-tech savvy as the U.S. What's happening in the world's largest democracy is absolutely fascinating. It's social/economic/environmental transformation before our very eyes of an unprecedented scale, and follows the same trajectory of all modernizing societies: idealized but parochial rural/agrarian to gritty but worldly urban/industrial, with investment (from abroad or at home) and infrastructure (highways, power plants) literally leading the way. Read Thomas Bender's *Toward an Urban Vision*, which profiles Frederick Law Olmstead and Charles Loring Brace, two figures who exemplified the shift in the U.S. in the early 19th century from rural to urban. As Gandhi and Ambedkar are to India, so Brace and Olmstead to America (or, more appropriately, Jefferson and Hamilton).

Main Street and the Internet

Perspectives on Place Blog
December 2005

Check out Keith Schneider's piece on internet sales
and downtown revitalization, http://www.mlui.org/
growthmanagement/fullarticle.asp?fileid=16965. In my
2000 book, *The Land That Could Be: Environmentalism
and Democracy in the Twenty-First Century*, I slammed the
emerging internet as just another excuse to shop, another
distraction from the important business of civic engagement
and environmental action. Fast forward seven years (I wrote
the book in 1998-99), and I'm all wet, or so it seems. As
Schneider points out, struggling merchants in downtowns
like Manitowoc, Wisconson, population 34,000, are using the
internet to boost their sales. E-commerce, Schneider writes,
"is enabling them to turn over their inventory much more
quickly, allowing store owners to add more products and
variety to sales floors. That, in turn, encourages more interest
and customer traffic, diversifies their revenue stream, and
contributes to downtown street life here and in other small
cities. . . . The [internet's] widening use by small retailers
is enlivening downtowns across the country by enabling
merchants to market niche products to a national and global
Main Street."

I love these kinds of paradoxes: the uber-tool of the
placeless, global age, the web, is restoring Main Street in the
heart of America. Go figure. Perhaps only time will tell, but
I'm thrilled by the idea that the internet could be a boon to
small business, downtowns and smart growth. On this score,
I'm happy to have been wrong.

Cosmopolitanism

Perspectives on Place Blog
January 2006

A great entre to the New Year is Kwame Anthony Appiah's piece in the January 1 *New York Times Magazine*. It's a very provocative and powerful analysis of what's wrong with claims of cultural preservation in the global age and, in many ways, speaks directly to those of us in the planning field. Local versus global, preserving what's special in our places versus inviting change and development, purity versus contamination. . . . Walmart versus farm fields, wind mills versus ridgelines, affordable housing versus open space.

Appiah:

Cultures are made of continuities and changes, and the identity of a society can survive through these changes. Societies without change aren't authentic; they're just dead. . . . Living cultures do not, in any case, evolve from purity into contamination; change is more a gradual transformation from one mixture to a new mixture, a process that usually takes place at some distance from rules and rulers, in the conversations that occur across cultural boundaries. Such conversations are not so much about arguments and values as about the exchange of perspectives. I don't say that we can't change minds, but the reasons we offer in our conversation will seldom do much to persuade others who do not share our fundamental evaluative judgments already. When we make judgments, after all, it's rarely because we have applied well-thought-out principles to a set of facts and deduced an answer. Our efforts to justify what we have done - or what we plan to do - are typically made up after the event, rationalizations of what we have decided intuitively to do. And a good deal of what we intuitively take to be right, we take to be right just because it is what we are used to. That does not mean, however, that we cannot become accustomed to doing things differently.

We often talk about "values" in our work, but I think land use debates are usually not so much about values as they are about habits, about doing things a certain way because that's what we're used to doing/seeing. This is what it means to be in the change business, which is the Foundation's business: We try to help communities see that in many respects their disagreements are not about fundamental values per se, but about perspectives and habits, and that these disagreements don't necessarily require a realignment of those values so much as they do an accommodation of changes.

I often refer to the debate about wind turbines here in Vermont as the new "civil unions," the issue that stirred Vermonters passions for several years in the late 1990s. The following from Appiah does a good job of explaining what I mean:

> In much of Europe and North America, in places where a generation ago homosexuals were social outcasts and homosexual acts were illegal, lesbian and gay couples are increasingly being recognized by their families, by society and by the law. This is true despite the continued opposition of major religious groups and a significant and persisting undercurrent of social disapproval. Both sides make arguments, some good, most bad. But if you ask the social scientists what has produced this change, they will rightly not start with a story about reasons. They will give you a historical account that concludes with a sort of perspectival shift. The increasing presence of "openly gay" people in social life and in the media has changed our habits.

And over the last 30 years or so, instead of thinking about the private activity of gay sex, many Americans and Europeans started thinking about the public category of gay people.

One of the great savants of the postwar era, John von Neumann, liked to say, mischievously, that 'in mathematics you don't understand things, you just get used to them.' As in mathematical arguments, so in moral ones. Now, I don't deny that all the time, at every stage, people were talking, giving one another reasons to do things: accept their children, stop treating homosexuality as a medical disorder, disagree with their churches, come out. Still, the short version of the story is basically this: People got used to lesbians and gay men. I am urging that we should learn about people in other places, take an interest in their civilizations, their arguments, their errors, their achievements, not because that will bring us to agreement but because it will help us get used to one another – something we have a powerful need to do in this globalized era. If that is the aim, then the fact that we have all these opportunities for disagreement about values need not put us off. Understanding one another may be hard; it can certainly be interesting. But it doesn't require that we come to agreement.

Substitute wind turbines for gays and lesbians and the same logic applies.

The Problem of Describing Trees

Vermont Public Radio
April 2006

I remember reading once that Norman Mailer, when asked about the complexity of American culture at a writers' conference, responded, "When I think about it, I start talking in a southern accent."

Mailer's characteristically brash reply has stayed with me through the years. Something about the idea of resisting the urge to analyze, of defying the desire to understand. Perhaps, however noxiously, Mailer was saying that, when the world throws you a curve ball, reach for a mint julep.

Whatever Mailer had in mind, I've been wrestling lately with the tension between my own need to explain the world, to describe and inquire into it, and my competing impulse to accept it as it is, on its own terms, mint julep in hand. It's my empirical, curious self facing off against my "It is what it is," "stuff happens" self.

We live, Wallace Stevens wrote, in "an old chaos of the sun." Stevens was right: the world is chaotic. It is a complicated system, with its countless moving parts and myriad dimensions, always changing yet repeating itself too. And we are its explorers, its diviners, its chroniclers, constantly seeking to bring order to the chaos, square the circle, tame the beast. And yet the system prevails, of its own momentum and mysterious logic.

Can it be that there are simply limits to what we can know and describe? Perhaps human art and science, even religion, as powerful and wondrous as they are, must yield to a greater, totalizing force called Nature or the Universe.

Not so long ago, I came across this short poem by Robert Hass. It's called "The Problem of Describing Trees."

The aspen glitters in the wind
And that delights us.
The leaf flutters, turning
Because that motion in the heat of summer
Protects its cells from drying out. Likewise the leaf
Of the cottonwood.
The gene pool threw up a wobbly stem
And the tree danced. No.
The tree capitalized.
No. There are limits to saying,
In language, what the tree did.
It is good sometimes for poetry to disenchant us.
Dance with me, dancer. Oh, I will.
Aspens doing something in the wind.

Walking the bottomlands near my house the other day,
I observed these selfsame aspens as they began to leaf out
and I thought of Hass's poem. I stopped dead in my tracks
and, with all my will, tried to avoid thinking about them,
analyzing them, as I so often do. Instead, with my eyes closed,
I started to meditate, freeing my mind of any thoughts or
feelings. I just was, there in the middle of the wood, a tiny
glimmer in the sun's chaos, and for a moment, a burden was
lifted, high to the tops of the trees.

Opening my eyes, I had to laugh. Standing there,
suspended in a soporific haze, none other than a mint julep
came rushing to my mind. Without the southern accent, I
might add.

Collective Action

Vermont Public Radio
August 2006

It's one of the great questions of political science, if not human civilization. Assuming that most of us act in our own self-interest most of the time, under what conditions can the collective good take precedence over individual gain? For a century scholars and policymakers have struggled to find an answer, with few practical results.

For those of us concerned about global warming, this question is particularly vexing. To confront it is to ascend a precarious high-wire, balancing on one side individual citizens, companies and nations, each in pursuit of what they think will help them get ahead – a bigger SUV, more coal-burning power plants. On the other side is the common good, not particular to any single interest and often elusive. There is no simple method for these acrobatics and, regretably, little precedent.

Until recently, much of human history has been a record of individuals simply striving to survive, to fend off predators and tyrants alike in a Darwinian cycle of kill or be killed. Our brains have been fine tuned by evolution to think in terms of our individual needs and to respond to danger only once it is upon us, not in advance.

Meanwhile, for thousands of years, people's belief systems were governed by a central premise: that our fate is not ours to determine but is instead the sole province of the gods or, worse, mere chance.

But with the Age of the Enlightenment 300 years ago, western civilization put forward a bold new proposition, that human beings could create their own fortune, alone and collectively, through their powers of will and reason.

We devised new technologies to improve our daily lives and communication, new laws to promote shared goals like peace and human rights, new institutions to celebrate our common bonds and heritage.

So why, then, three centuries into the Enlightenment experiment, are we still so unskilled when it comes to acting in advance on the common good?

It seems we've on recently arrived at a new evolutionary threshold, that the Enlightenment's promise of human emancipation and social welfare is still unfolding, still in the process of shaping our brains, beliefs and behaviors. After all, in evolutionary terms, 300 years is but a blink of an eye.

But perhaps a tipping point is not far off. More and more people are finding that the usual ways of doing things are no longer working and that a new mental model is needed, one in which the line between I and We, local and global, present and future is more elastic, less rigid.

I think Al Gore's recent movie, *An Inconvenient Truth*, is evidence of this, uniting everyone from suburban soccer moms to Fortune 500 CEOs in a shared concern about the environment and our future. Climate change, it turns out, is not so much a threat as an invitation, to a new commons known as Planet Earth and a new consciousness we call community.

Manchester Will Try Out Carbon-Balanced Living

The Burlington Free Press
March 2007

You might have noticed something different about last month's Academy Awards. Instead of a fleet of stretch limousines and outsized SUVs, many of the attendees arrived at the ceremony in a Toyota Prius, a carbon-friendly alternative. Meanwhile, the award presenters were not lavished with the usual decadent gifts but rather given a simple glass sculpture made in Vermont and a coupon certifying 100,000 pounds of carbon reductions to combat global warming. To top it off, the event was officially billed as the "Year of Carbon Balanced Living."

After more than two decades orbiting the public's consciousness, the issue of human-induced climate change has finally touched down, not only on the red carpet but almost everywhere else. And there's no greater symbol of the issue's potency than the carbon offsets showcased at the Academy Awards. Carbon offsets allow individuals and organizations to neutralize their climate change impacts by purchasing credits from others whose renewable energy projects help reduce greenhouse gases.

Not to be outdone by Hollywood, Manchester residents enacted their own version of carbon-balanced living when they debated purchasing offsets at the recent town meeting. They voted to forego what would have been the state's first municipal carbon offset program, opting instead to study the town's current electric and fuel consumption and ways the town can reduce its own greenhouse gas emissions. As one Selectboard member put it, "there's a lot we can do with cleaning up our own back yard."

The concept of offsets in environmental regulation is nothing new. Strategies for mitigating the effects of wetlands development and habitat destruction through the purchase of credits are well into their second decade, with mixed results. Likewise, emissions credit trading under the federal Clean Air Act is a mature, if still imperfect, system.

But none of these strategies has the Oscar-winning allure of carbon offsets. Which is why offset firms are popping up everywhere, some of them surfacing after years below ground, others newly flush with capital. What climate activist Bill McKibben calls the "Mother of All Environmental Issues" – global warming – has given birth almost overnight to an entire industry.

And that's where the celebrity of carbon offsets meets the reality. As with any rush – for gold in the mid-nineteenth century, for bandwidth in the late twentieth – the offset explosion has its hype, and its pitfalls. At least three come immediately to mind. First, because of the industry's youth, there doesn't yet exist a rigorous, scientifically-based set of standards for verifying the efficacy of any given offset program. Without a legitimate, third-party certifying institution, it's virtually impossible for consumers to know whether they're getting what they've paid for. Next, measuring the effects of a particular offset action is inherently challenging. The complex nature and sheer scale of climate change, and the fallibility of predictive models, make the impact, say, of a Vermont homeowner's purchase of an offset from a Chinese wind project very difficult to measure, let alone monetize. Finally, there's the problem of buying your way out of responsibility for your own carbon impacts. Offsets can too easily become an excuse for people to avoid changing their lifestyles, a convenient tool for the status quo

– the bigger house, the less fuel-efficient car, the coal-burning power plant. Factor in population growth and rising per capita energy consumption and the whole offset equation starts to look fishy.

The excitement generated by carbon offsets is a welcome trend. But before we anoint the offset industry as the planet's savior, we should consider Manchester's example and take a harder look at offset investments, making sure they deliver on their promises while encouraging responsible decisions, not only about offset projects half way around the globe but the ones right in front of us.

Collapse

Vermont Public Radio
July 2007

With the Vermont legislature set to vote on Governor Douglas's veto of the global warming bill, I've been thinking about the rhetoric surrounding the issue since the bill was introduced in January. From the editorial pages to emails, the important public policy at stake – how and on what schedule will Vermont reduce its reliance on fossil fuels – has often been overshadowed by sarcasm and soundbites. The real debate, if there ever was one, ceased months ago.

On the one hand, many of the bill's supporters chose to immediately put the spotlight on Entergy, whose Vermont Yankee nuclear plant would have been taxed at a higher rate under the bill to fund an expanded energy efficiency program. They couched their claims in a volatile mix of populism and nativism, portraying Entergy as a greedy out-of-state corporation hell-bent on getting while the getting's good while leaving Vermonters with tons of radioactive waste in the process. Omitting the fact that Entergy's the largest employer in southeastern Vermont, and is legally required to store its spent fuel on site, the supporters waged a campaign of corporate destruction against Entergy, with a clear message: If you're an out of state company and the legislature decides to turn against you, take cover.

On the other hand, the bill's opponents, led by Governor Douglas, engaged in their own brand of rhetorical mud wrestling. Until recently, the Administration hadn't bothered to put forward a legitimate global warming proposal of their own. The Governor seemed to ignore the bill's merits entirely and instead resorted to a diatribe against Big Government worthy of Ronald Reagan himself, as if the global warming bill were a proposal for some kind of welfare state. Offering little other than buzzwords, the Governor tried to beat the legislature at its own populist game, with Bureaucracy, not Entergy, depicted as the people's true enemy.

My point is not that politics can be a dirty business, or that our leaders are incompetent. It's that great social issues like climate change are tests of our political mettle, touchstones of who we are and what we're made of.

The geographer Jared Diamond argues that societies collapse when they stop thinking about their biological fate and focus only on their cultural survival, when they get so consumed with their belief systems and ideologies they starve to death, as the Norse did in Greenland as a result of deforestation and overgrazing. The Norse refused to eat fish because it was cultural taboo. Instead, they raised livestock until their soil eroded away and with it, their civilization.

With the global warming bill I believe we've gotten lost in our own ideologies. Big Bureaucracy, Bad Corporations – these are rhetorical abstractions. What's really at issue are tangible, finite things: maple sugaring, the ski season, the Northern Forest.

We need to stop behaving like the Norse and start acting like citizens. After all, Vermonters have risen to the occasion before. And besides, given our small, homogeneous population, if we can't do it, who can?

The New, Evolved Capitalism

The Boston Globe
July 2007

Carbon offsets have gotten a lot of attention in recent months. It seems everyone is jumping on the bandwagon, from hard-nosed CEOs to suburban soccer moms to boards of selectmen. And why shouldn't they? Offsets are a tantalizingly easy way to do what is otherwise difficult for most Americans: kick the carbon habit. Instead of having to change our lifestyles or corporate practices, offsets allow us to pay someone else to do it for us.

But offsets are more than just a clever tool to help us clear our collective conscience while we go about business as usual. They are a singular metaphor for capitalism and its offset equivalent, private charity. Offsets are to carbon emissions what philanthropy has been to American capitalism – a convenient though indirect way of mitigating the undesirable effects of a system and way of life we are unwilling to change through more direct means.

Whether a small family foundation or a massive charitable trust, the $300 billion in assets fueling the roughly 50,000 foundations in the United States today are derived from an economic system that has largely resisted changes meant to prevent the social, economic, and environmental harms the system itself produces. Rather than modify their business practices to account for these harms, industrialists, financiers, and others with great wealth have traditionally looked to philanthropy to help offset capitalism's adverse impacts, with a significant tax benefit to boot. As Henry Ford liked to say, "The system that makes my foundation possible is probably worth preserving."

This philanthropy-as-offset approach has proven a powerful

force in protecting the status quo. But if recent developments are any indication, the system is beginning to change. In the past several years, the line between for-profit business and nonprofit mission has started to erode. A new breed of social entrepreneurs has challenged traditional philanthropy and what they perceive as its limitations in effecting large-scale reforms. On one side, foundations such as Google and Omidyar, as well as nonprofits like the New Hampshire Community Loan Fund, have begun to invest in for-profit businesses with a strong social mission – software companies providing basic services to the poor, for example, or businesses that preserve good-paying jobs in struggling rural areas.

Meanwhile, private, money-making enterprises are incorporating social and environmental concerns directly into their business models. Honda and General Electric have recently launched bold environmental initiatives aimed at dramatically reducing carbon and other air pollutants from their products. Altrushare Securities, a for-profit brokerage firm, works to help economically distressed communities like Bridgeport, Connecticut, where it's based. And the list is growing.

These social enterprises are transcending the boundaries separating government, business, and nonprofits and forging a new meta-sector, what some are calling the "fourth sector." In the process, they are beginning to refashion American capitalism, long the nemesis of many reformers, into a, if not the, principal agent of social change.

Like carbon offsets, American philanthropy can be understood as an interim step in a larger process of transformation. Just as the solution to global warming ultimately requires each of us to dramatically reduce our carbon emissions ourselves rather than paying others to do it for us, we've come to understand that lasting, penetrating social change demands that our economic system, and the firms operating within it, integrate social needs directly into their business models instead of relying on charitable interventions after the fact.

In the fusion of commerce and the common good we are witnessing the birth of a new species of capitalism. For-benefit is starting to compete with for-profit as the dominant *modus operandi* of a growing corps of capitalists not content with simply reaping financial rewards.

But we are also witnessing something else, something equally profound. The emergence of fourth-sector firms demonstrates what is perhaps capitalism's greatest asset – its essential dynamism and capacity to change, to renew itself over time, however incrementally or begrudgingly, in response to new social conditions and markets.

In this sense, Henry Ford got it wrong. The system isn't worth preserving; it's worth evolving.

About the Author

A global leader in sustainability and social entrepreneurship, William Shutkin is the author of *The Land That Could Be: Environmentalism and Democracy in the Twenty-First Century*, which won a 2001 Best Book Award from the American Political Science Association, was selected as one of *Time Magazine*'s 2002 "Green Century" Recommended Books and was translated for publication in India. The legendary environmentalist David Brower described Bill as "an environmental visionary creating solutions to today's problems with a passion that would make John Muir and Martin Luther King equally proud."

The Public Press

We are The Public Press.
You are The Public Press.

Corporate media conglomerates continue to consume independents. While ownership consolidates, new book titles, specialized cable channels, and new websites proliferate. Amidst a din of commercial noise the bandwidth and coherence of available information is narrowing. Thoughtful authors find it more difficult to find publishers for sustained, original, and independent ideas at a time when technology is making it easier than ever to disseminate information.

The casualty is free speech.

The Public Press was founded in 2004 to protect freedom of speech "word-by-word." It is a grassroots organization, beholden only to its readers, its authors, and its partners.

The goals of The Public Press are printed below:

For more information, and to get a free subscription to the newsletter, The Page, visit: ThePublicPress.com.

Empower authors.

The Public Press puts the fewest possible filters or impediments between the creator and audience. The Public does not control the publishing process in the same way that a commercial publisher does. As a result there are stylistic and quality variations from title to title. The resulting books are like hearth-baked bread or handcrafted beer compared to more uniform, but less distinctive, products of commercial counterparts.

Treat authors as partners.

The Public Press is destined to become an author co-operative, where the authors are business partners with the publisher, not licensees paid a small percentage royalty on the sales of books. The Public Press offers an alternative to the traditional author/publisher model.

Leave the lightest possible footprint

Book publishing, historically, has been a notoriously inefficient industry from the standpoint of resource consumption. A book can travel across the country only to be returned, unsold, to its original point of shipment. The Public Press strives for economies of scale-small scale. New technologies have made available writing and editing tools, print on demand options, improved communications, and new sales outlets that make it possible for publishing to be a model of resource efficiency.

Shout from the highest tree.

The Public Press is comprised of a community of individuals who share certain values (such as an appreciation for independent thought and freedom of speech) but who may not share geography or demography. The success of The Public Press is entirely dependent on our ability to reach these people and to convince them to involve others. As opposed to our namesake counterparts, National Public Radio and Public Television, The Public Press receives no government funding.

Hear the voices...
on The New Village Green

"A small shift in one thing can produce big changes in everything."
Donella Meadows
author *The Limits to Growth*

THE NEW VILLAGE GREEN

BY THE EDITORS OF
GREEN LIVING

"*The New Village Green* is a testament that life endures, even flourishes... Do we know the factors that support community, enhance civility, and achieve sustainability? Read this book and find out."

Paul Freundlich
Founder and President Emeritus
Co-op America

"
Self-centered antiseptic paranoia, not the bacteria, is our enemy here."

Lynn Margulis
Biologist

"
Man is a part of nature, and his war against nature is, inevitably, a war against himself."

Rachel Carson
Silent Spring

"
We must therefore study the essential nature of the private enterprise system and the possibilities of evolving an alternative system."

E.F. Schumacher
economist and author of
Small is Beautiful

"
We don't need any middlemen to mediate between us and the Spirit."

Dave Smith
co-founder Smith & Hawken

A new book by the editors of Green Living Journal
Ask for it at bookstores everywhere
or buy online at
GreenLivingJournal.com/NVG